Sufism: The Nameless Faith

© 2016 Amany Daghesty, John Rychlicki III
Leilah Publications
All rights reserved.

Art: © 2016 Hamid Nasir

Table of Contents

3.   Chapter I...The Nameless Faith

23   Chapter II......................Qadr: Destiny and Predestination

31   Chapter III.............................Human Intimacy and Islam

49   Chapter IV.......Theology of Power: Wahhabism, Salafism, and Jahiliyya

56   Chapter V......Hashishiyya and Nusa'iri: Shadows of Syria and Afghanistan

67   Chapter VI.................Roshaniyya: the Illuminated Ones of Afghanistan

72   Chapter VII............Sufism, Freemasons, and the Illuminati

86   Chapter VIII............................Regenerating Islamic Faith

I. The Nameless Faith

The use of the word *Islam* is an inclusive term denoting a spiritual tradition originating in the revelations of the Qu'ran is contemporary, emergent in Western society in recent centuries. In the 20th century, historical and private accounts over encountering Islamic cultures in Britain and European countries often used the now-rejected term "Mohammedanism." When Islamic culture was in its original ascendant within the Arabian Peninsula, it was customary for its faithful to refer to the new spiritual tradition as a *din* ("religion"), characterized in Islamic terms as *din Ibrahim* (the religion of Abraham) or *din al-Haqq* (the religion of the Truth, God's own religion). It remains customary for many Muslims to refer to their faith, as *Din*, "the religion," as a mark of distinguished faith.

The Arabic word *Islam* denotes "submission" (revealing a linguistic root with *salam*, "peace"), and was used originally to refer to the mystical features of Muhammad's revealed *din*. The Hadith of Gabriel provides an effective exposition of the relationship between the experiential *Islam* and the general *din*. Umar Ibn Al-Qattab reports:
"One day when we were with God's Messenger, a man with very white clothing and very black hair came up to us. No mark of travel was visible on him, and none of us recognized him. Sitting down beside the Prophet, leaning his knees against his, and placing his hands on his thighs, he said: "*Tell me, Muhammad, about Islam.*" He replied: "*Islam means that you should testify that there is no god but God and that Muhammad is God's Messenger that you should observe the prayer, pay the alms-tax, fast during Ramadan, and make the pilgrimage to the House if you are able to go there.*" He said: "*You have spoken the truth.*" *We were surprised at his questioning him and then declaring that he spoke the truth. He said*: "*Now tell me about Iman.*" He replied: "*It means that you should believe in God, His angels, His books, His messengers, and the Last Day, and that you should believe in the decreeing both of good and evil.*" *Remarking that he had spoken the truth, he then said*: "*Now tell me about Ihsan.*" He replied: "*It means that you should worship God as though you see Him, for He sees you though you do not see Him.*" He said: "*Now tell me about the Hour.*" He replied: "*The one who is asked*

about it is no better informed than the one who is asking." He said: *"Then tell me about its signs."* He replied: *"That a maid-servant should beget her mistress, and that you should see barefooted, naked, poor men and shepherds exalting themselves in buildings."* Umar says: He then went away, and after I had waited for a long time, the Prophet said to me: *"Do you know who the questioner was, Umar?"* I replied: *"God and His Messenger know best."* He said: *"He was Gabriel who came to you to teach you your din."*

Umar's narrative is classified as an authentic hadith by *Ulema* (knowledgeable theologians), one of the most authoritative texts of Islam outside of the Qu'ran itself. The mystical nature of Angel Gabriel's to the Companions (*Sahabah*) of the Prophet and the ritualized, catechetical counsel, provide a concise realization of Allah's imminence and Mystery.

A man called Muhammad bin Abdallah ʿalay-hi wa-sallam, was born around $570^{A.D.}$ in a town called *Makkah* (Mecca) in the Arabian Peninsula. At the time of his birth however, his father ʿAbdallah was already deceased; Muhammad's mother Amina raised him up with the help of her extended family. Scholarly accounts from Ulema describe Muhammad as humble, honest, and conscientious in his youth, given to quiet reflection. In recognition of these traits, by friends and family, he was given the title *al'Amin*, "the trustworthy one."

Occasionally the young Muhammad would retire to a cave in the surrounding mountains of Makkah to meditate on the social and moral degeneracy around him and contemplate ways of counteracting them. Meccan society in decline in this period; in *jahiliyyah*, social degeneracy, oppression, bribery, and corruption, tribal warfare that led to many widows and orphans who were often left destitute. There appears to have been a breakdown in the basic social structure; In the midst of *jahiliyyah*, people like Muhammad were concerned about their condition and the social depravity from which they suffered.

Muhammad, did not become a total recluse, he was also a merchant and journeyed to trade, for example, to Damascus, Syria. On one of these trips, the Ulema tells us, he met a Christian monk called

Bahira, who foretold that one day he would be chosen by the one God, the God of Abraham, Moses, and Jesus, to be His prophet and Messenger to seal the revelations of God to humankind.

When Muhammad was about twenty-five, he married a twice-widowed 40-year-old woman, called Khadija, on whose behalf he had carried on some trade. With new financial and emotional security in his life, Muhammad dedicated his time more fully to reflection and meditation in his cave at Mt. Hira. One day, when he was about forty years old, around 610 of the common era, Muhammad heard a voice address him in his solitary cave:
"Recite, in the name of your Lord who created-
Created man from a blood-clot
Recite, for your Lord is bountiful
Who taught by the Pen
Taught man what he knew not."

The mystical intercession with Prophet Muhammad *ṣalla'Allāhu 'alehi wa'salaam*, is the starting point of Islamic mysticism. The divine intervention in the cave on Mount Hira is the mystic seal in a long mysterious tradition of Allah's intervention with humankind. Across the history of humankind, men, and women in cultures long-gone and empires whose ruins and exploits remain, have received intercessions from Allah, encouraging us to enact goodwill, and unconditional love. Far too often have these intercessions fallen to ridicule, linguistic misinterpretation (in the case of Christianity), becoming tools of war. *Humankind must separate the grace of God Mystery and religion from the wicked acts of twisted minds.*

It is said knowledge is nearer to silence than speech, hence many of the mystic traditions in each religion contain a deeper search and wisdom, often only *experienced*, and not found in sacred scripture or houses of worship. The quietist practices in religious traditions are part of the nameless faith, Muslims call *Sufism*. They are in harmony with Christian theory and draw nourishment from many traditions predating Christianity.

Islam is incomplete without Sufism, and Sufism lacks its mainstay, without Islam. The absence of self-reflective practices and meditative traditions in religions is potentially disastrous. Human beings misled by the fascinations and desires of the ego grow fanatical in the practice of religion, or alternatively fanatical in the obsessive fascination with glamorous mystic phenomena.

Religion is the notion of the supernatural; the world of mystery, the unknowable, or the incomprehensible. Religion is the border of the chimerical. By that is meant any order of things that goes beyond our understanding into the Mysterious. Intertwined with art, and sexuality, religion is one of many approaches to worship and fully experience the divine beauty of the universe.

Religion is a feeling of Mystery. Studying the full range of the world's religious traditions from Sufi Islam to Zen Buddhism, my research and published writings focus on syncretism in human spirituality. The many traditions I involved myself in wholeheartedly from Yoga, Tantric secrets, Buddhism, Unitarianism, to the blackest occultism and Kabbalah led me on a digression from an ordinary religious believer, following conventional faith.

The wayward paths of disbelief in the divine Creator, Artist, Architect, and Causer of the universe lead humankind to emotional and spiritual darkness. The whisperers of witchcraft and occultism view religion as obsolete and destitute; would they surrender the human condition to endless spiritual anarchy?

Prodigious minds contributed throughout the centuries to the pillars of art, classics, literature, music, and the sciences; they are the custodians of the Nameless Faith, a spiritual movement of enlightenment and artistic understanding of the human condition and humankind's destiny. These prodigies are found in Christian, Muslim, Buddhist, and other mystic world religious foundations. Coincidently, the sneaking whisperers (Surah 114) would see centuries of untold enlightenment in religious classics, arts, & literature, committed to diabolical ruin. These listed occult orders and "movements" are infectious to logic and reason; they are only products, easily marketable in a self-published digital world that knows little distinction between research and ranting.

Occultism often attracts narcissistic personalities who have a grandiose sense of self-value, and they consistently overestimate and overvalue their endowments. They exaggerate their accomplishments and are boastful, arrogant, and pretentious. Many have real talents and abilities, most are simply legends in their own mind tending not to test themselves in natural echelons. Their identities are codependent on their emotions, expending critical amounts of energy guarding against feelings of shame, humiliation and protecting them from criticism.

It is common for them to be easily wounded and oscillate between guarding feelings of superiority, against having anyone finding out how inferior they feel compared to their delusions of superiority. Occult personalities of sneaking whisperers are very status oriented and prefer to be with admirers or others who can maintain and inflate their feelings of artificial prodigy.

These megalomaniacs have a strong sense of entitlement, often denied them in professional, social, and academic environments preferring to focus their feelings on lacking qualities. They incapable of taking responsibility for their behavior while ignoring ensuing consequences and prefer to blame others for their moral and professional failures.

Their poise is artificial, as they expend maximum efforts in denying, hiding, and lying about their moral failure. Relationships are regarded either as a danger to their artificially superior status, or as a booster, enabling approval or serving as an audience. While they may be very good at showing concern for others, especially within a group setting, it is a sham. They lack real compassion and emotional depth, too preoccupied with their grandiose fantasies.

They do not see the world clearly; because they are blinded by feelings of entitlement, and delusions of grandeur. They remain unaware of their neuroses, unaware their minds are lost in delusion. Such perceptions descend into paranoia, and feelings of depression, aggression, and recrimination. When these individuals do not resolve issues of entitlement, they are physically unhealthy, unattractive, and unintelligent, unable to apply intelligence professionally and artistically.

Their strategies for coping moral and artistic failure is to increase their level of controlling behavior. Some become eccentric and withdraw from life into esoteric pursuits, joining occult orders and working their way up artificial magical rankings where they can verify that they are chosen, unique, and special. Some even provoke intense persecution and crucifixion of sorts to prove their grandiose neuroses. They have extreme difficulty in accepting the proposition that nature is arbitrary, capricious, and beautifully chaotic. It is difficult for them to accept themselves and life without a story of grandeur and entitlement.

Our attention must remain on the religious and artistic geniuses. The genius of Ibn al'Arabi, Rumi, Da Vinci, Mozart, Beethoven, even the rebellious minds of Nietzsche, de Sade, al-Hallaj, and Sayyid Qutb would not have manifested without the spiritual intercessors in the Christ, Muhammad, and countless other prophets and divine messengers unnamed.

Religious life, exclusively pursued, does tend to make the person exceptional and eccentric. Experience of divine perfection and beauty is a prime characteristic of consciousness, a mystic singularity, experienced with Allah (*tawhid*). Along with *tawhid*, enlightenment alone places the individual on a new plane of existence, making him almost a member of a new species within humankind.

With *tawhid,* the mystic enlightenment comes in may be called a sense of immortality, a consciousness of eternal afterlife, not a conviction that one shall have this, but the realization that one has it already. The fundamental religious elements of *tawhid* and *salat* (prayer) in Islam is that in prayer, spiritual energy, does become active in a transference of energy from the natural world to the supernatural, and spiritual work is affected. Sufi Islam, occupied with personal destinies and keeping contact with the only absolute realities we know, must necessarily play an eternal part in humankind's history.

It is in mystic surrender to this will, what Allah has created in divine order, that we find a lasting peace.

The balance between the exoteric and esoteric religious life for Muslims was circumspect in early Islam, giving rise to confusion by Ulema, the custodians of orthodoxy. The Holy Qu'ran states that 'God is Light' and Sufism is an inherited tradition that identifies light, *nur*, with Essence/Being, *wujud*. Sufi mystics like Ibn Arabi also spoke of the evanescence of Allah; Allah can never be truly seen and nothing may encompass Allah.

For the orthodox Muslim, Allah is separate from *wujud*, contrasted with Darkness, *zulma*, Nothingness, as the cosmos is seen as an emanation of light between the two. Ibn Arabi teaches that His Eternal Position in the Divine Presence is in the World of Souls and Light. This is a timeless dimension. Allah brought into existence the pure darkness that is opposite this light. *Nur* is in the position of absolute non-existence opposite absolute existence. When He brought it into existence, that light flowed onto it with an essential out flowing with the help of nature.

Creation is the *barzakh*, connection, between light and the unfathomable Void. Light, like Essence, is at once ontological and epistemological, associated with perception and knowledge. Sufi knowledge is a light that Allah throws into the hearts of men and women. This is the root of Ibn Arabi's mystical ontology, in that true knowledge is *tawhid*, knowledge of the reality of Allah, a matter of opening and unveiling, *futuh al'mukashafa*. The veils of existence are phenomenal causes and effects, or forms *suwar* that obscure the Light of the First Cause, of Allah.

In the philosophy of Ibn Arabi, the names are a connection between Allah, his Essence, *Haqq,* and the created worlds. The mystical doctrines, such as *dhikr* (remembrance) of Sufism shelter the heart of Islam. The sufiyya are mystics, many predating Islam, but for whom Islam has become the eternal refuge, unaffiliated with interpreting the Qu'ran in a legal and theological manner. Sufis were in essence the first psychologist of Islam, while Ulema were the first legal scholars. Sufis sought to approach the human condition in Islam from an emotional, spiritual, and intuitive means, whereas the Ulema approach Islamic life on rational, logical, and theological positions.

Al'Ghazzali sought to reconcile these two positions in Islam, but it is debatable whether his success was limited. The Ulema and sufiyya offer intellectual alternatives to presenting Islam and its revelations to non-Muslims. The scholars of the Ulema are held in high academic standards to those whom would join their exclusive community. Ulema are the rationalists of Islam, sustainers of the *ummah*, (community) serving as guides. Sufiyya are religious adherents to an inclusive approach to Islam that has enchanted non-Muslims especially Westerners with metaphysical prejudice. There exist many metaphysical secrets within the practices of the Sufis sects such as the Aissawa and Naqshbandi Orders.

In Sufi doctrine, certain lineages, *tariqahs* ("chains," or "brotherhoods") construe *Islam, Iman,* and *Ihsan* as three points of psychic and spiritual evolution. The Muslim, the adherent who exercises *Islam* becomes oriented to *Shari'ah*, which while it literally means "road," is ordinarily translated as "Law." The *Mu'min* (one who exercises *Iman*) embarks on *tariqah*, the mystical chain of spiritual enlightenment. Moreover, the *Muhsin*, adherent who exercises *Ihsan*, acts from the state of *haqiqah*, the ultimate spiritual reality, where there is only contemplation with the divine.

(photo: *La tâ`ifa du muqaddem Haj Saïd Berrada*, courtesy http://confrerieaissawa.free.fr)

Sufis have ensured the perpetuation and security of Islam as a religion. Without the sufiyya, Islam would, in my opinion, lack the livelihood of the revelation of the Qu'ran and become a tomb rather than a vehicle of human spiritual enlightenment. Sufism is a mystical college whose true origins lay not in the Qu'ran or the *Din al-Muhammad*; the true origins of Sufism remain untraced or dated.

Sufism is at home in all religions yet is sheltered by the fruit of Islam. Sufism is the secret teaching of all ages, within all religions. Sufi, like "Zen Buddhist," is just a moniker. Artists, poets, and musicians were the chief disseminators of Sufi thought. Sufis have always insisted on practical spirituality.

Faith in God is unsurprisingly the first and foremost article of *Iman*. The *Din al-Muhammad* is the purest monotheism to emerge from the Abrahamic tradition, and it affirms God as consummate and distinct from the universe that is his creation. According to the *shahadah* or declaration of faith, God is one, an idea expressed in the theological concept of *tawhid*, or unity. Sufi mystic teaching is a rich spiritual tradition that articulates Islam. From *suf* derives the term *tasawwuf*, literally to put on a woolen garment, figuratively implying an adherent to Sufism, or Islamic mysticism.

The Quran contains 99 sacred names of Allah, the "most beautiful names, *al asma'ullah al husna*. In the philosophy of Ibn Arabi, the names are a connection between Allah, his Essence, *Haqq*, and the created worlds. The mystical doctrines, such as *dhikr* (remembrance) of Sufism shelter the heart of Islam. Mystical experiences are ineffable and the final authority to interpret the experience resides solely in the devotee whom experiences the realm of the sacred. The mystic in any religion is one whom penetrates into the mysteries and nature of the divine and the human condition.

The sufiyya are mystics, unaffiliated with interpreting the Qu'ran in a legal and theological manner. Due to extensive insights into the nature of the human condition, the Qu'ran, and Hadith, the Sufis were in essence the first psychologists of Islam, while the Ulema were the first theologians. Sufis sought to approach the human condition in Islam from emotional, spiritual, and intuitive notions, whereas the Ulema approach Islamic life on rational, logical, and theological conceptions.

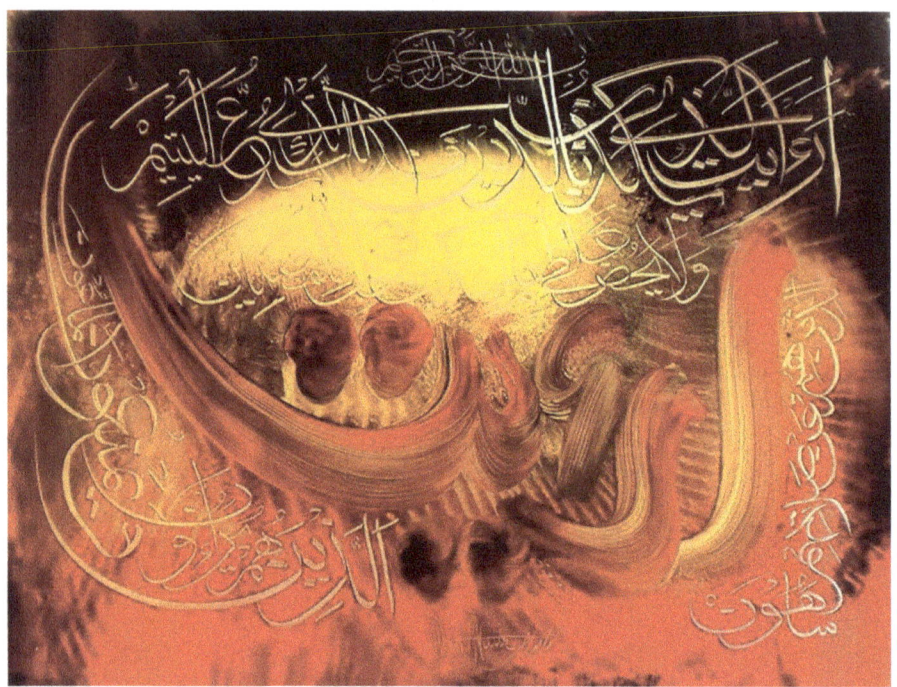

Metaphysics are of no use without practical illustrations of prudence that nothing can intoxicate; these poetic illustrations are supplied by popular legends, music, and fables. Surrounded by modes of digital exposure on a global scale, Sufism retains its mystic quality without Internet dissemination. Sufism is the grand demarcation between the subconscious mind and religion. Sufism's *Sunnah* (Arabic: 'clear path') is for the freedom of ideas, intolerance against cruelty, hypocrisy, and religious persecution; their opposition was to injustice and political crime. Their stories were the subject of divine intoxication, love, and human suffering.

As Sufi Muslims read the Qu'ran with studious meditation, hidden meanings, infinite, and unfathomable, of the Holy Word awaken the mind. Sufis call this *istinbat*, a sort of intuitive awakening; a mysterious current of divinely revealed knowledge into hearts by repentance filled with sacred study of Allah, and the tide of that knowledge upon the humble and studious mind. Even if Islam had been inexplicably shut off from contact with foreign religions and philosophies in its early stages, a form of mysticism would have arisen, for the seeds were already planted.

Sufi mystical poetry is the biography of humanity. Their poetry defies fortune and outlives the world's calamities. They are an eternal college surviving all empires, conquerors, kings, and revolutions. Sufism is a comfort to the broken hearted, immortalizing the poet, consoling the mind's silent tragedies. These courageous souls paint visions of divine beauty and ecstasy across the hearts of humankind.

The Sufis regard the universe as a projected and reflected image of Allah. The divine *Nour* (light), coursing forth in a series of emanations, falls at last upon the Void of Not, every atom of which reflects some divine creation of Allah. Consequently, the divine attributes of love and mercy are reflected in the form of heaven and the angels, while the terrible judgment of wrath is reflected in the form of hell and the shayateen (devils).

Humankind reflects all the attributes, the terrible, as well as the beautiful; we are an epitome of heaven and hell. As evil is really evil, the absence of unconditional love and goodwill, it emanates from the whirling sentient Void of Not-Being, the "Shaytan," accursed one who hungers eternally for the wickedness of human souls.

Atheists and disbelievers object and state that if Allah created evil, then the Creator is an accessory to evil, containing the element of the created overspreading Void of Evil, the attributes of the Shaytan – and yet does a painter retain the defect of an unattractive art piece in himself? Sufi Muslims show us that no religion has a monopoly over truth. Sufism is the nameless faith offering the relief of human misery and spiritual evanescence. For a Sufi, the World of Souls, and Light is the point where life begins and where it ends.

Besides a divine order and beauty, the Qu'ran also reveals earthly, interpersonal love in a few different contexts. It declares that Allah, s.w.t., has united the disunified peoples of the earth using the bond of love: *"for ye were enemies and He joined your hearts in love,*

so that by His Grace, ye became brethren..." (Surah 3:103) It also describes love as the bond sanctioning marriage: "*He created for you mates from among yourselves, that ye may dwell in tranquility with them, and He has put love and mercy between your hearts,*" (Surah 30:21) and the energy that motivates humans to procreate: "*It is He Who created you from a single person, and made his mate of like nature, in order that he might dwell with her in love. He giveth them a goodly child.*" (Surah 7:189-190)

Sufis are known for their commitment to the fine arts, ghazal poetry, and Zen influencing anecdotes in spiritual tales called the Mathnawi. The love of this world stems from *tawhid*, (oneness), and a love of the divine presence a Muslim recognizes in all life. Specific mystic states identify the egoistic and social ills of this world. Ḥaqiqah is a degree attained by Muslims, through continuous contemplation and inward devotion, rise to the true perception of the nature of the visible and invisible in this world. Ma'arifah is where a Muslim receives divine communication with Allah.

Humankind also has a latent evilness inside that is friends with the evilness outside the soul. We have a soul and our souls come from paradise; from the Divine, imprisoned by the ego and its desires. It escaped the heavenly abode in Paradise (*Jannah*) and then the rule of *wilaya*, the rule of divine authority, is that if they escape and they arrive in this world, applies to those who seek Allah to govern their life in this world. When a Muslim experiences this spiritual awakening, the practice of that religious opening is to ask; *"What does God want from you, when He opens your heart?"* Allah is going to open your heart; to take off the blindfold around the soul, opening reality.

When a Muslim comes into Islam, and experiences the deeper mysteries of Sufism, the realization is that one is not outside of Allah's kingdom; we are in *Allah's* Kingdom. As the Lord's Prayer of the Christians is spoken, '*Thy Will be done, Thy Kingdom has come,*' and it is in our heart as it is in His Heaven. Often we cannot understand this because we love this world too much, we are attached to its sickness, and we are attached to drinking, its drugs, its power games, its pornography, its money, wealth, and properties.

Humankind ends up so deep into that dungeon; we cannot imagine why nobody else loves this dungeon? Yet we go through so much struggle, so much trauma, much heartache, and spiritual darkness. When we emerge from this dungeon and spiritual crucible, and Allah says, "I have a request for you, go back in, but this time you go in supported as a Muslim.

Many people suffer in violent loneliness, whether through heartache, addiction, sex, or abuse, we fail to understand. Blindfold yourself. It means admit to yourself; you cannot know. When we begin to think we know what is best for our body, mind, and soul, we remove the blindfold. The only way to reach Allah's *nur* is to remove the spiritual blindfold over our minds, over our souls, and come to an understanding of the nature of ultimate reality, of *tawhid*. *Tawhid* means to remove the blindness of ego, to efface oneself and enter into that ocean of Divine love, Divine mercy, and Divine grace.

When one removes the blindfold of *fitnah* and *jahiliyya* (disorder, and ignorance), at this point the Divine Light will begin to reveal itself within ones ill-stricken heart. With the blindfold of ego and false realities around our minds and soul, we have no guide warning us how dangerous our illusions and lies could become. This is when ones faith is tested, even new reverts to Islam. Crucibles of faith, to take away all the false gods, all the false desires that we may know or not know of that exist; usually occur after one makes Shahadah.

When Muslims pray, prayers are purely out of love of Divine Presence, love for Sayyidina Muhammad s.a.w., and all great souls that are holy. Prophets, guides, and religious intercessors come into our lives and begin to point out that they can see what we cannot see, they sense what we cannot sense, because Allah guides the faith of these people. The Prophets and guides, the Imams, our teachers, and families, guided after their own crucibles through Islam, see the idols that we are worshipping, is our possessions, the false idol of wealth and worldly fame.

Many wealthy Muslims have these possessions, and you find them to be praying but they are actually praying to secure and prolong their idolized wealth. Muslims think often we are in favor with Allah because money comes in, business comes in, health is restored, and life is good. Then the crucibles that Allah in His Divine Presence gives is that, turn your eyes and hearts towards the prophets and saints and rightly guided, you will face crucibles as they faced them. And Muslims are tested with their life and monies, and family and with everything to see what your faith is truly made from.

We are unable to see with the blindfold of ego and the *dunya* that with difficult times, wealth is pulled, one loses the will to make prayer. Depression sets in, and the thoughts come, "O I am very depressed, I cannot pray right now." Alternatively, a crucible as a death or calamity comes, we say "I cannot pray now," or "I do not wish to pray right now." If these thoughts are realities, then it was not Allah that one was worshipping; it was the idolatry of things.

The Prophets and our guides show you signs within yourself what you need to change. One simply has to watch the news, drive down the street and read a newspaper and we see how wickedness surrounds us, how Islamophobia and anti-Muslim violence grows, how fitnah overspreads in violent minds. People who lend their minds to bad desires, to their egotistic will and to their desires based on those wants, they inflict harm, and they inflict lies and oppression upon people. All that matters is the quality of our light; the purity of our soul on the spectrum of Allah's light.

The Prophets and their inheritors the Saints, the guides in our lives are all asking us to contemplate that if we love Allah, what can we offer to express that love? We cannot offer good deeds alone, we cannot offer sacrifices to idols, and we cannot offer anything from this world. Allah reveals through the rightly guided Prophets and the Qu'ran, 'If you truly love me, then love the Creator, the Supreme Being of Beings and your neighbor with what I gave you; your Free Will.' And all the rightly guided Prophets and Saints were teaching this basic trust.

The Lord's Prayer says, "*Thy Kingdom come, thy Will be done on earth as it is in Heaven...*" Allah's will, not our will be done, because our will is simply a blinding tool of our ego, a barrier psychological and spiritual health. Allah knows what human minds are incapable of imagining. Prophet Muhammad (s.a.w.) is teaching us, rightly guided saints are teaching us, that we must submit in grace to a Creator who intervened with humankind and loves us enough to have fashioned a special destiny (*qadr*) for humankind. Through that grace in submission, we will reach towards Divine Presence; we reach into *tawhid* (oneness).

We often do not understand truths like this; rarely do we contemplate the deeper meanings of tawhid and divine presence. Many Muslims and even non-Muslims think they have a right to come and describe Allah, s.w.t., assuming their relationship with Allah is personal and close enough that Allah would speak for them. Although there are some who tell the truth about this, be aware that many of those who claim it are delusional, falling into misguidance.

If we do not know our selves, how can one know Allah? And if you take *dhikr*, and sit quietly contemplating, Allah will inspire within our hearts an awareness, a question that breaks down the *nafs*, (ego, personal desires); 'How could we possibly assume we know Allah, if we do not even know the beast within us, although we are never separated from our minds and bodies?' Realize that we do not understand the main motif of the nafs, desires and impulses, our temper and egotistical reactions to situations.

Muslims must look deep enough in our hearts, and often enough to even ask why we act the way we act, are we kind enough, is our character good, are we tolerant enough of non-Muslims, are we becoming fundamentalist, and radicalized? For us to answer firmly means we can know ourselves and master our good character. So how can we say we know and take remembrance of Allah's Divine Presence, above all prophets and saints, majesty and might? We must know the beast within, before we know Allah and even speak from Allah's wisdom and grace. Such *dhikr* personal honesty and courage for correct self-contemplation is called *Tafakkur*. These traits are reflected in our Prophet Muhammad, s.a.w. Unlike the creations of angels, humans, and djinn, Prophet Muhammad was divested of all ego and wants, dissolved in the Presence of Allah.

II. Qadr: Destiny and Predestination

Destiny or "power" in Islam is *qadr* and *taqdir*; derived from Q-D-R. It is *the making manifest of the measure (kamiyya) of a thing,* or simply *measure*. Allah's *taqdir* of things is in two ways, by granting *qudra* (power) or by making them in a particular measure and in a particular manner, as wisdom requires. An example of *taqdir* is the creation of the sperma of man, out of which grows man only, not any other animal. *Taqdir* is therefore the law or measure, working throughout the whole of creation; and this is exactly the manner *qadr*, and *taqdir* are used in the Qu'ran. *"Exalt the name of your Lord, the Most High, Who created and proportioned and who destined and then guided."* (87:1-3)

Every part of creation has a taqdir, a 'measure,' and it is Allah who creates and measures all allotted destinies: *"Who created everything, then ordained for it a measure (taqdir)"* (25:2), *"Surely We have created everything according to a measure (qadr)."* (54:49) *"And the sun runs on course toward its stopping point. That is the determination (taqdir) of the Exalted in Might, the Knowing. And the moon - We have determined for it phases, until it returns appearing like the old date stalk of the Mighty, the Knowing. And as for the moon, We have ordained (qaddarna from taqdir) for it stages."* (36:38-39) The words *qadr* and *taqdir* occur 60 times in the Qu'ran.

Humankind is included in the creation; our *taqdir* is consequently the *taqdir* of Allah's entirety of creation. *"Of what thing did He create him? Of a small life-germ He created him, then He made him according to a measure (qaddara-hu)"* (80:18-19) These verses on *taqdir* show that in the context of the Qu'ran, taqdir is a universal law of God, applying to both mankind and the sustained universe; a law extending to all the worlds, the galaxies, stars, the planets, and strange souls inhabiting them.

The interpretation of *taqdir* as 'predestination' partly comes from a misguided analysis of good and evil in Islam. The following verses in the Qu'ran clarify the idea of Allah's power: *"Yet, when a good thing happens to them, some people say, 'This is from God', whereas when evil befalls them, they say, 'This is from thee O fellow-*

man!' Say: 'All is from God.'" (4:78) *"What, then, is amiss with these people that they are in no wise near to grasping the truth of what they are told?" Whatever good happens to thee is from God; and whatever evil befalls thee is from thyself."* (4:79) *"Behold, as for those who are bent on denying the truth -- it is all one to them whether thou warnest them or does not warn them: they will not believe. God has sealed their hearts and their hearing, and over their eyes is a veil and awesome suffering awaits them."* (2:6-7)

Dr. Allama Iqbal has written so much about the concept of *taqdir* that it would entail a complete book for us to make *bayan* (clarity) on his views concerning the difficult issue of predestination and Islam. Iqbal summarizes thusly, *"The world of plants and animals is subject to taqdir. A Momin is subject to nothing except the orders of Allah, s.a.w. (i.e., Quran)."* Muslims these days, especially converts who are subject to radicalization, use the excuse of *'taqdir'* in order to justify their prejudices and intolerance towards non-Muslims. The divine Firmament of Allah, *Amr*, is beyond human comprehension. No one can grasp the meaning or purpose of Allah's divine realms of providence. Human beings cannot know how Allah created the universe into existence from the Firmament.

The subtle power of *taqdir* is a secret hidden in one word Allah has willed. Human beings can change the course of their life, and then the taqdir changes consequently. The Sufis say a human being comes from dust, and return to dust after this life, then even the wind will scatter you and carry you wherever it wishes. If a human being becomes like a stone, developing a hardened heart and mind, many obstacles will break against you. If a human being becomes like a dewdrop then destiny is an abyss for that lost soul, as the sun will wipe you out of existence. And, if you become like an ocean, your *taqdir*, will know power and deepness.

If a human being falls into an abyss, lost in their ego and crucible, he/she should not resign to fate and blame their *taqdir*, their destiny. Allah has written this in one's fate and that one cannot do anything about it is often the cry of those who cannot understand *taqdir*. The Qu'ran does not encourage this fatalist attitude. Allah, s.a.w., says in the Quran, *"It is a fact that Allah, s.w.t., does not change the condition of a people unless and until the individuals (composing that society) change what is inside of them."* (13:11) Since Allah does not force *taqdir* of change on human beings, it is up to us to act on the spiritual desire to change. Metaphysics, which confuses the human and divine will, where souls claim to create their own laws, puts human beings back into an abyss of insanity. Human beings do not create our own laws, our own realities, we are not gods.

The entire universe operates under the laws created by Allah that a small percentage of human beings understand. Human beings are responsible for their own actions if performed under our own free will, our personal *taqdir*. One cannot escape the consequences of one's actions. Whatever we sow in the field of career and profession, relationships, family, love and war, we are subject to our *taqdir*, which is what we reap. Iqbal writes in his only English translated book: "*Thus there is nothing static my inner life; all is a constant mobility, an unceasing flux of states, a perpetual flow in which there is no halt or resting place.*" (page 38, ed., published jointly by the Institute of Islamic Culture and Iqbal Academy of Pakistan, 1989)

Allah created all time and space, a continuum of conscious awareness for human beings, not a string of separate instants in flux, creation in time and space is an organic continuum where past operates with our choices in the present, and the future yet to be traversed in the *qadr* Allah designs for all possibilities. Time and space are the organic whole of Allah's *Al-Khalaq* (creation), described in the Qu'ran as a complete destiny. *Qadr* in the context of destiny is not an unrelenting force; it is the full realization of all possibilities created according to Allah, s.w.t.

Taqdir can if perceived as a "divine right," damage the psyche of the Ummah, applied to the divine sovereignty of Muslim Caliphs, Kings, Sultans, and even Muslim institutions of learning and theology. If catastrophes of economic disparity and poverty strike families and starving children, then it must be Allah's taqdir, while wealthy Princes dine and feast in mansions within Saudi Arabia, Kuwait, and other countries. Misunderstandings of predetermination cause apathy. We all have free choice, and once this choice is made, Allah has already given result, what Iqbal calls the law of *Mukafat-e-A'mal*. What one sows, one shall reap.

The Greek philosophers, Socrates (470-399^{BC}), Plato (427-347^{BC}), and Aristotle (384-322^{BC}) concentrated on the moral tendency of humankind to find the truth of inherent goodness in the human condition. Medieval Christian dogmatism led man to despair as he had no freedom to enquire about the authority of the Church and had to suffer for Biblical original sin. Renaissance theologians like Francis Bacon (1561-1626), Rene' Descartes (1596-1650) and Leibniz (1646-1716) focused on rationalism of creation and divine order, than on the spirituo-ethical state of the human condition.

The philosophers of the Christian Enlightenment centered their dogma on the material progress and happiness in the world of cause and effect, ignoring the role of metaphysics and spirituality. Humanity was subject to divine determinism, which, in consequence, restricted the human realm of activity. Islam, the primordial and revealed religion of Allah for all-encompassing guidance of humankind, resolves the problem of free will and determinism in totality.

Questions of *taqdir* often struck the minds of some of the Prophet Muhammad's companions (*sahabah*), leading to commentary and discussion (*ahadith*). It was, however, through the syncretistic interaction with and influences of the other religions and mystic philosophers that the question of destiny became the subject of theological debate and discussion during the Umayyad period of Islamic history.

During Abbasid age, the *Mu'tazilah* (theologians) and *Ash'ariah* schools reached their philosophic heights, and undertook the theology of *qadr* and determinism. The Mu'tazilah relies on rationalism and revelation some respects yet on the whole it maintained its special character through the doctrines of *Tawhid*, the unity of Allah s.w.t. In their doctrine of *Tawhid*, the Mu'tazilah designate humanity as the author of our own actions. If not, then we cannot be called free and responsible for our own actions. Free will is basic to the whole of religion and its revelations.

Alternatively, the Ash'ariah make a distinction between *khalq* (creation) and *kasb* (acquisition). According to them, Allah is the creator (*khaliq*) of actions and humankind is the acquisitor (*muktasib*). Therefore, Allah is the creator of human actions and humanity the acquisitor. Allah creates in humankind the power to do an act and gives the ability to make a free choice (*ikhtiyar*). Abū Ḥāmid al-Ghazzali, a medieval Islamic theologian, elaborates on free will and determinism in the light of his description of the three worlds: the physical world (*alam al-mulk*), the mental world (*alam al-jabrut*), and the spiritual world (*alam al-malakut*) vis-a-vis the design of free will.

Al-Ghazzali believed impressions and ideas, which he calls *al-khwatir* condition, our senses and affect the human heart. Whatever the will intends or resolves that first comes to it as an idea leads to human action. The action then operates through the stages of inclination or impulses; a process of intellect, or conviction, (*i'tiqad*) and finally volition. To Ghazzali the conviction and volition of human will is not under the complete control of humankind, because they are affected by Allah's providence.

We have the freedom therefore, of forming our character, producing acts but at the various stages of its operation subject to the factors, which are not under our full control. The impressions and ideas that motivate humankind to conviction and volition arise from Allah's creation. However, when the impressions (*al-khawatir*) translate into acts of will, we enjoy the phenomenon of choice (*ikhtiyar*).

Freedom of choice comes from responsibility of actions. It is the responsibility of accepting the Trust (*amanah*) of Allah that provides individuals to choose between various alternatives. Choice arises from convictions and volitions in the phenomenal world where we choose one course of action and discard the other. We exercise choice because of appropriation for it. About the Trust of Allah, the verse of the Qu'ran clarifies: *"Verily, We offered the trust to the heavens and the earth, and the mountains but they declined to bear it and shrank from it. But man undertook it."* (33:72)

Theologians like Iqbal reconcile free will and determinism or destiny of God. To him, there is no contradiction between free will and predetermination. Human destiny is a limitation to divine activity. Yet this limitation does not rob us of Allah's infinity and grace. It is limitation that makes Allah intelligible to the finite egos, which appropriate private volition to act and are not, therefore, outside Allah. Allah is the source and free will is organically related to Allah. Allah is the ultimate determining power to guide and direct all free-willed acts.

Humankind's free will is limited by Allah who is infinite. We are not free like Allah. Free will opens for us the vast field of divine destinies (*taqdirat*). Humankind cannot create like Allah, yet we have the capacity to change our *taqdir* with Allah's guidance and grace. In spite of our limitations, we can affect change in our own creative life and in our environment. This is Allah's sphere of creation and freedom to choose our destiny.

We owe free will, our existence, body, soul, and life to Allah. It is not physical or rigid predetermination or fatalism. Humankind is free to deliberate the possible alternatives and become responsible for our own convictions and actions. Islam and the revelation of Allah is the spiritual destiny of hope and enthusiasm rather than a ruthless compulsion. The enigma of free will and determinism has remained baffling to humankind, and the Islamic treatment of *taqdirat* and *qadr* illustrate the appropriation of humanity's vital role in the world of Allah's power and creation.

III. Human Intimacy and Islam

The relationship between the erotic and death is quite relevant to the discussion of mysticism in Sufi writings such as Jalaluddin Rumi's Mathnawi. I discuss themes of the erotic in Sufi mysticism by providing specific examples. I will survey specific figures within the Sufi tradition I am most familiar. To examine the subject is unavoidably exhaustive and would require a familiarity with over 1,300 years of literary and artistic development. This is beyond patience of the reader and the limited scope of this book.

There is already quite a range of expression of the sexuality in the history of Sufism and any of my additions would do a disfavor to current research. My survey of Sufi eroticism will extract specific motifs and, when applicable, relate them to their possible influences and development. As Sufism is highly metaphorical and esoteric, interpretation will be difficult, especially themes of sexuality. I will survey a few specific themes in Sufi mysticism.

Logically, I will discuss Prophet Muhammad ṣalla Allāhu ʿalay-hi wa-sallam, as the starting point of Islamic mysticism; Rabi'a, as the founder of the theme of Sufi love; al'Hallaj, whose writings are the classic voice of impassioned union; al'Ghazzali, as the clear-headed systematizer and reconciler of mysticism with orthodoxy; Ibn al'Farid, as the composer of what is perhaps the greatest erotic love poem in all of Sufi literature; Ibn al'Arabi, as the supreme philosopher of the erotic in the Sufi tradition; and Rumi, as the exponent of love best known to the West.

The earliest detections scholars have of the theme of the erotic in Arabic poetry predates Islam. Poetry was the primary form of literature, the main form of artistic expression, of the jahiliyya period, circa 500-622[A.D.]. While there were a few different types of poetry, the qasida, or ode, was the only completed literary type. The qasida had an invariant structure; a Bedouin would stumble upon the remains of a desert camp and sing of its desolation. His loneliness would inspire him to recall his fondness for those who had once encamped there, and he would describe with great nostalgia the strength of his affection for his beloved and not infrequently would describe her in detail.

This section of the poem is called the nasib, 'erotic prelude.' Ibn Qutayba describes the nasib: here the poet, virtually always male, "bewailed the violence of his love and the anguish of separation from his mistress and the extremity of his passion and desire." Part of the Bedouin-poet's motivation in including this was to win the hearts of his hearers, since the song of love touches men's souls and takes hold of their hearts. After the nasib, the poet would praise his camel and the fortitude of the Bedouin people, and following all of the above would begin the body of the ode, usually a panegyric to his patron or a tale of battle.

The qasida was so central to Arab culture that, the image of the poet weeping at the memory of his lost love is considered the main expression of pre-Islamic literary themes with matters of love and sexuality. His detailed descriptions of her were sensual and conveyed appreciation of moral beauty.

It was the revolutionizing influence of Muhammad, s.a.w., that inspired the development of a spiritual side to erotic poetry. Unlike founders of certain other religions, Muhammad, s.a.w., figures relatively modest in the theme of erotic mysticism. He was sometimes an object of love for the later Sufis, and certainly was often a focus of Sufi Ghazzalis {love sonnets}. The Western student of Islam might be surprised to see the strong mystical qualities attributed to Muhammad, s.a.w. Students tended to overlook is the quality of mystical love that Muhammad's, s.a.w., followers feel for him.

However, his influence in themes of the erotic is much more literarily diminished than that of the founders of some other religions is for their followers. For example, some medieval nuns meditated on the body of Christ with a concentrated devotion approaching erotic fascination, an idea unusual to Islam. The Qu'ran elevates love to one of its central motifs. Muhammad, s.a.w., writes frequently of the Quranic promise of Allah's love for those who lead righteous lives and the threat that love will be withdrawn should his followers be unrighteous.

Besides this divine Platonic love, the Qu'ran also reveals earthly, interpersonal love in a few different contexts. It declares that Allah, s.w.t., has united the disunified peoples of the earth using the bond of love: *"for ye were enemies and He joined your hearts in love, so that by His Grace, ye became brethren..."* (3:103) It also describes love as the bond sanctioning marriage: *"He created for you mates from among yourselves, that ye may dwell in tranquility with them, and He has put love and mercy between your hearts,"* (30:21) and the energy that motivates humans to procreate: *"It is He Who created you from a single person, and made his mate of like nature, in order that he might dwell with her in love. He giveth them a goodly child."* (7:189-190)

There is only one mention in the Qu'ran of things erotic, namely in the story of Joseph and his master's wife Zulaika (12.24) where did she desire him, and he would have desired her. The women of the cities later gossip that he had "inspired her with violent love." (12:30) Nothing comes of their mutual desire, though, and this particular incident in the tale of Joseph appears not to have stirred mystical experiences.

It was left to the Sufis to connect the themes of Islam and the erotic. The mystical thought of the first century or so following the Prophet was inspired by the same elements in religion that motivated Muhammad. At its basis, was the fear of God and of the Wrath to come on the Day of Judgment.

Some scholars have diminished the role of Qu'ran in Sufism's development, postulating rather that it must have grown out of relations with Nestorian and Monophysite Christians, mystical Judaism, or even Buddhist and Hindu influences. It was in the writings of Rabi'a Al'Adawiyya that the *mysterium fascinans* began to take precedence over the *mysterium tremendum*. Rabi'a is the first to introduce the theme of love into Sufism, not just the pious love of God and the brotherly, tranquil love of one's fellow Muslims, but also an erotic love whose only goal is unity with Allah s.w.t..

Though Rabi'a's love of Allah s.w.t. and Allah, s.w.t. only could be quite coldly ascetic at times, she often shut her windows to the flowers in spring in order not to be distracted, theologians treated her fairly. In a religion and an age where the role of women was anything but positive, where one text was careful to define Rabi'a as a man before praising her and others went so far as to declare women to be created from the sediment of the sins of demons, Rabi'a's name quickly became a synonym for praiseworthy women.

To this day, a woman is praised by being called a second Rabi'a, and the poet Jami said, *"If all women were like Rabi'a then women would be preferred to men."* Rabi'a was, first, a lover of Allah s.w.t. Her love for God was so absolute that she refused to compromise it by loving another human, even the Prophet himself. "I belong only to Him," was her answer to Hassan al'Basri's marriage proposal.

Indeed, her love of Allah s.w.t. was so pure-minded that she rejected even some of the most basics tenets of her religion, as expressed in her famous prayer; *"O God! If I worship Thee in fear of Hell, burn me in Hell; and if I worship Thee in hope of Paradise, exclude me from Paradise; but if I worship Thee for Thine own sake, withhold not Thine Everlasting Beauty."*

As Rabi'a clearly introduced the theme of erotic divine love, she uses limited symbolism of love in her poetry. Her descriptions of love tend to be very chaste. It was a major Sufi figure, al'Hallaj, who inherited most profoundly Rabi'a's legacy. He was much less meticulous about using traditional and non-sexual imagery, and was more explicit about the goal of union. The erotic love that inspired Rabi'a was, an intimate love, a love for which God has not asked and for which He will not recompense the lover.

This sense of Allah's love was strengthened in the thought of many later Sufis, such as Abu'l'Husayn an'Nuri, who spoke of being a lover 'ashiq of God and felt a love so overreaching that the orthodox considered him likely to be tempted to commit blameworthy acts. To defend himself against those who objected that a self-sufficient entity could not feel the sort of longing implied by passionate love 'ishq, Nuri stated that the lover is kept at a distance from Allah s.w.t..

Nuri's takes Nuri's erotic love to its logical conclusion, namely the union for which passion longs contemporary, Husain ibn Mansur al'Hallaj. Rabi'a loved Allah s.w.t. who she wrote of as her true Lover, a being who created her and yet was distinct from her. Al'Hallaj, though, often has been interpreted as loving a God who was identical with himself. Inspired by Qur'anic verses such as *"He who hath given thee the Qur'an for a law will surely bring thee back home again,"* (28:85)

Al'Hallaj wrote; "*I have become the One I love, and the One I love has become me! We are two spirits infused in a (single) body.*" This sense of tawhid, of a complete immersion of the lover and the beloved, led Sufi poets to speak of Allah s.w.t. in very amorous terms. For al'Hallaj, divine union is consummated in the amorous nuptial where Allah s.w.t. ultimately rejoins His creature, and in which the latter opens His heart to His Beloved in intimate, familiar discourse.

Al'Hallaj's writings represented a marked distinction from other, non-religious poetry of the time. The ideal of Baghdadian high society at the time, he states, was the search for sensual ecstasy, often inspired by what he terms *femmes de luxe*, women who were 'professional idols of beauty' who functioned 'to stimulate people's desire for aesthetic diversion.' The presence of human beauty inspired an awareness of divine beauty, as if one's attraction to the human was intentionally transmuted into an attraction to Allah s.w.t..

Similarly, al'Hallaj would at times speak of the relationship between the mystic and God as being like that between lovers. Al'Hallaj explains his insight into tawhid, portraying Allah s.w.t., as playing some kind of erotic game, in which Allah s.w.t., presents the mystic with a series of veils that must be lifted, one by one. This sensual revealing, and hiding, titillated the mystic and tricking him into being attracted to divinity that the mystic rationally understands must ultimately remain unapproachable.

Al'Hallaj in no place uses imagery that could be misconstrued as referring to human sexuality. The mystery of erotic Union is celebrated in verses free of any trace of the imagery of solely sexual love. Al'Hallaj's care in not to using profane imagery seems not to have saved him from the misunderstandings of the Orthodox clerics. One of the three main reasons he was executed was for his crime of zandaqa, 'thesis of divine love.' Al'Hallaj was fresh in the mind of a mystic who followed him by two centuries, Abu Hamid al'Ghazzali (d.1111).

In many ways al'Hallaj made Sufi mysticism quite suspect in the eyes of much of the orthodox Sunni Muslim community, a status al'Ghazzali was determined to rectify. He succeeded; for he is regarded as not only the reconciler of orthodoxy and the heterodox Sufism, but has even been called by clerics 'the greatest Muslim after Muhammad s.a.w.' His influence in Islam seems in many ways to be analogous to that of Augustine's in Christianity. Their similarity is especially marked in their approaches to the interface between sexuality and mysticism.

Al'Ghazzali, like Augustine, was emphatic about the good of sexuality and marriage when practiced in their proper social strata, and the evil of both when misused. He writes; *"Know that marriage is one part of the way of religion, like eating food...God created the womb. He created the organ of intercourse... No intelligent person will miss what Allah means by this Marriage as created and sanctioned by Allah has another necessary component: desire...God created appetite as a deputy responsible for encouraging people to marry."*

However, it was clear to al'Ghazzali that human lusts can become ends in themselves. *"Marriage was made permissible for procreation, not for the sake of satisfying ones' appetites,"* he writes. A personal love of Allah, which al'Ghazzali calls 'the highest of all things," belongs in a position superior to any and all other forms of love. If this love does not "conquer a man's heart and possess it wholly," or at least "predominate in the heart over the love of all other things, then the lover is in spiritual danger."

Al'Ghazzali's thought on eroticism in Sufism comes out most clearly in his discussions of mystical union with Allah s.w.t., and the manifold theological confusion around it. He was made exemplary literary use of erotic imagery as metaphors for divine ecstasy. He does not entirely discount this theme, yet rather cautions clearly that one not confuse the intent.

As regards the erotic poetry which is recited in Sufi brotherhoods, to which both orthodox Sunni and Shi'a clerics objected, remember that, when in such poetry mention is made of separation from or union with the beloved, the Sufi, who is an adept in the love of Allah s.w.t. applies these passions to separation from and union with Him.

Al'Ghazzali defends Sufism against the complaints of those who, believing all Sufis to be as heterodox as al'Hallaj, objected to discussions of union with Allah s.w.t. He makes this quite clearly in his epilogue to the Ninety-Nine Beautiful Names of Allah s.w.t., where he exhaustively explains what al'Hallaj was touching on by declaring his soul and Allah s.w.t. to be united. Al'Ghazzali lightly criticizes al'Hallaj without actually disagreeing with him. He concludes that al'Hallaj is not blasphemous, rather only unwise in proclaiming a mystical truth that could be misleading to the uninitiated.

In his Deliverance from Error, he explains that the fault lies, not in the attempt to attain union Allah s.w.t., but in describing it incorrectly. The mystics progress to a "higher stage" where, instead of beholding visions, *"they come to stages in the way which it is hard to describe in language; if a man attempts to express these, his words inevitably contain what is erroneous."* What these mystics really achieve, he says, is nearness, *qurb* they may call it inherence *hulul*; union *ijtihad*, or connection *wusul*, but these are erroneous.

There is certain ambivalence in al'Ghazzali's defense of al'Hallaj; I am left with the impression that, though he consistently denounces al'Hallaj as unwise and mistaken, yet he privately does not reject al'Hallaj's claims. I will refrain from drawing conclusions about al'Ghazzali's feelings on the use of sensualism and erotic imagery, for I again detect certain ambivalence between his exoteric philosophy and what seem to be his personal beliefs. He explains that music and dancing can induce states of ecstasy that "fan into flame whatever love is dormant in the heart, whether it is earthly and sensual, or divine and spiritual."

If love in one's heart is true, then "it is perfectly lawful, nay, laudable in him to take part in exercises which promote it," but "*if his heart is full of sensual desires, music, and dancing will only increase them and are therefore unlawful.*" Later, he explicitly links Qur'anic recitation and erotic poetry as valid ways to stir the emotions. His ambiguity is caused by the fact that some of his texts were written for the uninitiated public and others for his circle of students, and his explanations differ accordingly depending on whom he is addressing.

The resolution is simply that the worldly appetites, for al'Ghazzali, are admirable if motivated by a divine form of love, "the senses were created to spy for the intellect. They were to be its snare through which it might know the wonders of Allah's handiwork," and blameworthy if motivated by worldly satisfactions only, "*the pig is appetite…through covetousness the pig invites to indecency and abomination.*"

There are two figures from the thirteenth century I must survey together. Though the philosophies of the Egyptian poet 'Umar Ibn al'Farid {d. 1235} and the Spanish theosophist Muhyiuddin Muhammad Ibn al'Arabi {d.1240} are unalike, they do share other similarities besides being contemporaries; each has attracted the fascination of Westerners to a great extent, and, more pertinent, each uses allegories of the erotic to an extent unmatched by almost any other Muslim mystic.

Ibn al'Farid is, after al'Hallaj, the mystical poet of the Arabic language who has attracted the most attention by Muslims and Arabs. Indeed, R. A. Nicholson devotes a full third of Studies in Islamic Mysticism, the first major work on Sufism in English, to The Odes of Ibn al'Farid. In his odes, which unquestionably form the climax of classical Arabic mystical verse, al'Farid sings some of the most direct and romantically heartfelt love poetry to be found in the whole of Sufism. The earliest source within Islamic history of the erotic poem is, as mentioned above, the prelude to the qasida, the subject of which was the poet's earthly love, his celebration of her beauty, his longings for her, and a mourning of her absence.

As we have seen, the early Sufi expressions of love tended to focus on a love that was spiritual only, even though the uninitiated often misunderstood it to be an organic one. Ibn al'Farid's writings bridged the two extremes of chastity and eroticism, and this is perhaps a part of the reason that they achieved such popularity; both the mystic and the worldly person could find meaning and aesthetic pleasure in his poetry. His greatest work, the *Ta'iyyatu'l kubra*, or "*Lesser Ode rhyming in T*," is the greatest example in Sufi literature of such poetry. It can be read both as a mystical text and as a celebration of earthly courtship.

Al'Farid set out to celebrate the divine lover in his works, not only the earthly, lover. The greatest mistake one can make in interpreting his poetry is to assume that the poets exclusively refer in their love poems to sexual love between lovers, in context to the eroticism in Solomon's Song of Songs. My interpretation of the *Ta'iyyatu'l kubra* is substantiated by the fact that Ibn al'Farid once said, "*Had I wished, I could have written two volumes of commentary on every verse of it.*"

Though the common person may read his verses simply as love poetry, many of Al'Farid's contemporary mystics shared his interpretation of the work. Ibn al'Farid's commentator, Nabulusi, explains that in every erotic description, whether the characters are male or female, and in all imagery of gardens, flowers, rivers, birds, and the desert, Ibn al'Farid refers to the Divine Reality manifested in phenomena, and not to those phenomena themselves.

The lengthy *Ta'iyyatu'l kubra*, 761 verses, uses the device of a running narrative interspersed with dialogue to describe the phases of mystical experience through which one passes in attaining oneness with Allah, describing the nature of that oneness. Unlike many other examples of esoteric discourse, Ibn al'Farid's symbolism was not so much a mask used to hide what would be dangerous to express in plain speech, but was a literary instrument of imparting mystical truth.

I will recap the basic elements of the poem. Though it is a lengthy presentation by Sufi literary standards, the poem is very relevant to Sufi erotic literature. The poem opens in a way reminiscent of the jahiliyya poetry; the narrator complains of his sufferings in the path of seeking his beloved, his loneliness, and his longing to be with her.

"*I drank love's strong wine, and when my sobriety was ended, I sought union with her my beloved. And I said, from my state of ardent love and suffering, bestow on me your glance. I feel a passion that only tears betrayed. Anguish hath sorely oppressed me, and emaciation hath laid bare the secret of my true being. But thy beauty ordained that I should endure, for when one is ensnared by Beauty, methinks his soul even from the most delicious life is gladly rendered up to death. I swear by the firm pact of love between us that thou art the desire of my heart and the end of my search. Everything in thee is the source of my fascination, and I never was bewildered until I chose love of thee as a religion.*" (Verses 1-83)

The Beloved answers him, telling him he is insincere and presumptuous. He is not really in love with her, but just with himself. "*Another's love hast thou sought and hast taken the wrong path. To those who are rightly guided the straight road unto me is plain, but all men are made blind by their desires. Cease, then, pretending to love, and shun the quarter of union: tis far off, and was never reached in life, and lo, thou art living. If thou art sincere, die! Such is Love.*" (84-102)

The poet objects that, no, such a death is his truest wish, for it is through such a humiliation that true honor lies: "*By my life, though I lose my life in exchange for her love, I am the gainer; and if she wastes away my heart, she will make it whole once more.*" (v. 121) He now turns to his audience, and explains that this beloved has truly become the focus of his spirituality. *"'Tis my being crazed with love of her that makes me jealous of her, and my spirit is rapt in ecstatic joy towards her. Whilst I prayed mine eye was seeing her in front of me, and to her I address my prayers."* (verses 144-152)

Yet, in a style very reminiscent of al'Hallaj, and Rabi'a the Lover and the Beloved long to be one. *"Both of us are a single worshipper who, in respect of the united state, bows himself to his essence in every act of bowing. And I saw that I was indubitably she whom I loved, and that for this reason my self had referred me to myself."* (v. 153-163) What Ibn al'Farid desires in this bond is not the ontological tawhid of which al'Hallaj was accused, but rather an ecstasy, a forgetting of one's Self. It seems as if the discontinuous selves have now attained a state of marriage, from which they work as a team. *"I sought to approach her by sacrificing myself, and she drew me nigh. And with entire disinterestedness, I put behind me, any regard for myself. Through her, not through myself, I began to guide unto her those who by themselves had lost the right ways; and 'twas she that really guided them."* (v. 168-174)

Now the poet begins to explain as well as he can just what the nature of this union is. It seems as though he is trying to explain *baqa'*, or subsistence, the state which follows the above *fana'*, extinction. *"I had been enamored of her, but when I renounced my desire, she desired me for herself and loved me. And I became a beloved, nay, one loving himself. Through her I went forth from myself to her and came not back to myself. In the sobriety after self-effacement I was none other than she, and when she unveiled herself my attributes became hers and we are one."* (v. 204-215)

After more discussion of the nature of this union, Ibn al'Farid seems to explain that God manifests himself in beauteous forms for the sake of tricking humans into following this, the right path. *"The charm of every fair youth or lovely woman is lent to them from Her beauty. It was only because she clothed herself in the form of beautiful phenomena, and her lovers supposed that these phenomena were other than she, that they loved her. Every lover, I am he, and She is every lover's beloved, and all lovers and loved are but names of a vesture."* (v. 242-264)

Ibn al'Farid continues his exposition of *ijtihad*, emphasizing in passing the importance of not abandoning the shari'a, the path of law, in favor of the mystical quest. He then pauses to offer a fifty-two verse eulogy of his beloved and her beauty. It serves as a beautiful lyric interlude, later returning to the topic with a fascinating presentation and celebration of the physical senses as vehicles for divine awareness. *"Let me tell thee the mystery of that which my soul received secretly from my five external senses and communicated to my inward senses. My thought beholds the Beloved with the eye of my fantasy, and I wonder at my drunkenness without wine, and am thrilled in the depths of my being by a joy that comes from myself, and my heart dances, and my spirit is my musician. Every organ of sense unites me with Her, and my union includes every root of my hair."* (v. 409-417)

The rest of the poem deals with Islamic doctrine and theology, such as the unreality of metempsychosis and the importance of faith, and meditations of the nature of reality. I wish to draw attention to some specific, yet various, aspects of the *Ta'iyyatu'l kubr* that are of importance to Sufism, relating to its mystical discourses. One of the most unusual aspects in the *Ta'iyyatu'l kubr* is the physical tone with which the poet speaks in places and the organic nature of the symbols.

Not only does he cast the mystical drama in human terms, but also he even celebrates the human senses and shows that they can act as conduits for spiritual ecstasy. Throughout the entire poem, al'Farid uses physical symbols such as clothing and veils, dressing and undressing, hiding and veiling, the comeliness of faces, and a catharsis of the transcendent Beloved with the physical senses. His use of the feminine pronoun, *hiya* and *ha*, is very unique. I find it acceptable from a literary and spiritual scope to connect his theme of eroticism with the use of feminine imagery, without reducing the interpreter to a standpoint of sexism.

Remember that Ibn al'Farid's audience past and present, was and is likely to interpret the text in such a way; that is, to see it as erotic if but for no reason other than that the motifs are feminine. This is significant because such motifs are unusual. Feminine imagery will not be seen as no more unusual than the use of masculine imagery, because Masculine imagery, e.g. Allah s.w.t. as He and the poet a man, is the norm.

The linguistic use of a feminine pronoun immediately calls attention to itself, as it refers in different points in Sufi poetry to Allah s.w.t. I find a considerable amount of Mystical Arabic poetry that employs the feminine pronouns hiya and ha, yet in these instances the pronoun refers to a grammatically feminine object, such as nafs, the soul.

Applying the feminine pronoun to Allah though, is not a case of grammatical necessity. Another important aspect is the dramatic element of the poem. However, it is not a dialogue between lovers directly, since the Beloved only speaks once (verses 84-102), we can see much indirect dialogue. Al'Farid's 'confidant' speaks to him in verses 24-25, in nonverbal speech, a kind of auditory intuition into the poet's mind, "as though the Recording Angels had come down" (verse 25).

I also find a few points throughout the poem where Al'Farid seems to be addressing the reader. This dialogue gives me the impression of reinforcing the theme of intimate interaction between the lover and the beloved, culminating in their mutual ecstasy, and in their living as one soul, almost as an officially married couple. Ibn al'Arabi uses gender imagery in a similar way to Ibn al'Farid; both envision a dialogue between the soul and Allah s.w.t. through the analogy of a dialogue between a male lover and a female beloved.

Contrary to the poet Ibn al'Farid, Ibn al'Arabi is a philosopher. Al'Arabi expands this mantle beyond mere poetry and offers readers an ontological explanation of the cosmos and a soteriological explanation of encounter with Allah s.w.t. In short, he sexualizes the cosmos. At this point I will survey the theme of romanticized mysticism in the of Ibn al'Arabi's literary style with themes of the erotic in the worldly plane, and its impact on his theology.

Human relationships inspired Ibn al'Arabi to incite rousing erotic imagery and motif, specifically the relationship between lovers, especially women; the fondness the Prophet felt for women, and a decisive tryst Ibn al'Arabi himself had with a young woman. There is a famous hadith where Muhammad s.a.w., states that Allah s.w.t., a love for perfumes and women, and joy in prayer gave him.

Ibn al'Arabi makes extensive use of this hadith in the final chapter of his *Bezels of Wisdom*, where of his reverence for women stems on this proclivity of Muhammad s.a.w.. He believes that Muhammad s.a.w., did not merely feel an attraction to women, but even pointedly raised awareness in early Sufism about the general concept of femininity in certain locutions of grammar. *"Then the*

Apostle goes on to give precedence to the feminine over the masculine, intending to convey thereby a special concern with and experience of women."

This verse is significant, he explains, because Arabic language usually has masculine gender prevail. One must be particular not to interpret this youthful fondness as an emotional one only, al'Arabi goes on to explain that Muhammad s.a.w., also loved *"the aromas of generation in women, the most delightful of perfumes being experienced within the embrace of the beloved."* Since Prophet Muhammad s.a.w., is the model of enlightenment for all of humanity, he concludes, *"love for women is obligatory."*

Al'Arabi also had such a decisive tryst with a young woman that was extensively influential on his thought. A Shaikh had a daughter, 'a particularly lissome young girl,' and Ibn al'Arabi states he *"observed with care the noble endowments that graced her person."* He took her as a model for the poems in the present book, which are love poems. She became a conscious inspiration for his literary work, for he soon says, *"whatever name I may mention in this work, it is to her that I am alluding."*

The sensual attraction I believe Ibn al'Arabi felt for women was not confined to his imagination or his mystic visions, for I find he does celebrate sexual intercourse. *"When a man loves a woman, he seeks union with her, that is to say the most complete union possible in love, and there is in the elemental sphere no greater union than that between the sexes."* The high class that Ibn al'Arabi places on physical charms and sex should not be fathomed that his life was extravagantly lascivious.

On the contrary, his intention is tantric-like; he elevates sex to a spiritual tradition and goes so far as to implicitly create, if, his entire cosmology on the model of sexuality. I do not believe that Ibn al'Arabi is prescribing sexual activity as a means of achieving spiritual realization, yet in certain points of his poetry, he is doing exactly that, and I cannot fault him.

Al'Arabi venerates the procreative role of sex, stating, "The relation of woman with man is that of Nature with the Soul. Woman is the medium through which children appear just as Nature is the medium through which bodies appear." He is not just reiterating his beliefs; rather, he immediately follows this remark with the statement that *"There can be no Soul without Nature and no nature without Soul."*

Al'Arabi follows the above discussion over *"delightful aromas"* of the woman's skin during sex, he interprets Qur'an 24:26, the word of *tayyib*, to mean, *"sweet-smelling," thus giving the meaning as 'sweet-smelling women, tayyibat, are for sweet-smelling men.'*

I conclude that by his mystical interpretation of sexuality, this prescription of erotic aromas is most necessary to understanding eroticism in Sufi poetry. Regarding the young woman, we discussed earlier, Ibn al'Arabi wrote that all names in his poem were to be taken as references to hers. His mystical interpretation of sex refers to religious attributes in erotic imagery, manifested as phenomena, nonexistent without a transcendental love for the Beloved; Allah s.w.t., the one truly Beloved of all humankind.

IV. Theology of Power: Wahhabism, Salafism, and Jahiliyya

The intolerance and fundamentalist convictions of Wahhabism-Salafism are an aberration to Allah's s.w.t. grace revealed in the Qu'ran. Lack of progressive social & economic development projects, entrenched U.S. and European manufactured authoritarian regimes (Egypt's Mubarak, Iraq's Saddam Hussein, Libya's Muammar Qadhafi), the inability to respond effectively to Israeli belligerence in Palestine, have provoked and identity crises in Muslim countries giving rise to ideological fundamentalist Islam.

A long line of puritan Islamic ideology has been passed down for generations in the Muslim world. Ibn Taymiyya (1268-1328) is considered to be one of the most important figures in the development of puritan radical ideology. Taymiyya, wishing to resurrect the purity of early Islam, derided deviations from the Quranic social vision. His views, which often opposed the Ottoman government, eventually led to his arrest and imprisonment.

A central figure in the growth of Islamic puritan ideology is Muhammad ibn `Abd al-Wahhab (1703-1792), a Saudi theologian and co-founder of Saudi Arabia. Wahhab demanded purification of the Islamic world condemning European and non-Muslim society. Believing European and Christian influence to be corruptive to Muslim purity, Wahhab encouraged his followers to revive a purist Quranic vision of Islam.

Wahhab's theology transformed into a religious movement called Wahhabism. Since its inception, Wahhabism has been financially and politically supported by the Saudi royal family. Wahhabism's strict rejection of the liberal and fine arts, ascetic vision, and religious interfaith tolerance has held great zeal for contemporary puritan Muslims.

Any form of moral and ethical philosophy not dependent on the Quran, any attempts to interpret divine law from a historic or contextual perspective were zealously rejected and seen as 'sciences of the devil' by Muhammad ibn `Abd al-Wahhab. All this behavior, Abd al-Wahhab denounced as *bida* (forbidden).

The royal Al Sa'ud family in the late eighteenth century aligned politically with Muhammad ibn `Abd al-Wahhab, and the tribes of Najd. Their strategy inspired like the I.S.I.L. D'aesh today; bring the peoples whom they conquered into total social and political control. The Wahhabi campaigns were designed to instill fear in Muslims and non-Muslims living in the Ottoman Caliphate.

In 1801, the Wahhabis allied with the Al Sa'ud family attacked the city Karbala in Iraq. They massacred thousands of Shi'ites, including women and children. Many Shi'ite sacred archaeological sites were destroyed, including the shrine of Imam Hussein, the martyred grandson of Prophet Muhammad s.a.w.

A British official, Lieutenant Francis Warden, witnessed the massacre at the time, wrote: "*They pillaged the whole of it, and plundered the Tomb of Hussein... slaying in the course of the day, with circumstances of peculiar cruelty, above five thousand of the inhabitants.*" Osman Ibn Bishr Najdi, the historian of the first Saudi kingdom, wrote that Ibn Saud committed a massacre in Karbala in 1801. Najdi zealously narrated that massacre saying, "*we took Karbala and slaughtered and took its people as slaves, then praise be to Allah, Lord of the Worlds, and we do not apologize for that and say: 'And to the unbelievers: the same treatment.*"

In 1803, Abdul Aziz entered Mecca, which surrendered under the reigns of terror and panic, with Medina soon following the same fate. Muhammad ibn ʿAbd al-Wahhab zealots demolished historical and archaeological sites. By the siege's end, they had destroyed centuries of Islamic architecture near the Grand Mosque; centuries later, the I.S.I.L. D'aesh would bring the exact same fate upon Iraq and Syria.

In November of 1803, a Shi'ite assassin struck down King Abdul Aziz avenging the massacre at Karbala. His son, Saud bin Abd al Aziz, succeeded him, and continued the Wahhabi scourge of Arabia. Ottoman rulers, however, could no longer just sit back and watch as their empire was devoured piece by piece. In 1812, the Ottoman army, composed of Egyptians, pushed the Wahhabi insurgents from Medina, Jeddah, and Mecca. In 1814, Saud bin Abd al Aziz died of fever. His unfortunate son Abdullah bin Saud, however, was taken by the Ottomans to Istanbul, where he was gruesomely executed. A witness in the city reported seeing him paraded in the streets of Istanbul for three days, hanged and beheaded, his severed head fired from a canon, and his heart cut out and impaled on his body.

Wahhabism survived the Ottoman purge and flourished in the following centuries in the Kingdom of Saud, receiving royal backing. With rising oil wealth, Saudis aggressively promoted and infused the Muslim world with the zealotry and puritanism of Wahhabism and Salafi theology. To Wahhabism and Salafists, their theological doctrines of *ijtihad* are not a school of Islam, it *is* Islam. Salafism was founded in the late nineteenth century by puritan zealots Muhammad `Abduh al-Afghani and Rahid Rida.

Methodologically, Salafis are identical to Wahhabist thought. Both schools are anti-intellectual, intolerant of interfaith dialogue and non-Muslims. Like Wahhabists, Salafis idealize the era of the Prophet, s.a.w. and the companions, ignoring the development of Islamic culture and history. Salafism and Wahhabism became indistinguishable thanks to an Egyptian theologian, Sayyid Qutb.

One of Qutb's peers, Mawlana Abu'l-A `la Mawdudi (1903-1979), helped shape Qutb's Islamist ideology. Mawdudi was a Pakistani journalist, politician, and the founder of the Islamist group *Jamaat-I-Islami*. Mawdudi focused the Islamist rejection of secularism and European-American society, on a narrower rejection of imperialism and the infiltration of "Western" culture in Islamic lands. Believing western economics, politics, and culture to be a threat to the survival of Islam, Mawdudi, and his *Jamaat-I-Islami* encouraged the resurrection of a strictly Islamic society, under the dictates of *Shari'ah*.

Even though Taymiyya, Wahhab, and Mawdudi were all influential in Qutbian thought, Qutb's enormous popularity arose from the egalitarian eloquence of his works, and his ability to incorporate his own, unique views with Islamic zealotry. More zealous and subversive than his predecessors' purist ideologies, Qutb's zealotry would become the foundation of terrorist groups promoting violence and cruelty.

Qutb's critique of jahiliyya is rooted in his belief that Islam can become the foundation for an all-embracing ideology of social and political organization. To implement the Islamic vision, Qutb offers a theology of liberation that would remove the ambiguity about the supremacy of Islam and return the affairs of the Egyptians and indeed all Muslims to the tenets of Islam and bring about *hakimiyyat'Allah*, the rule of God.

Sayyid Qutb claims that contemporary societies, both Islamic and non-Islamic, are in a state of jahiliyya resembling the 'state of ignorance' of Islam in pre-Islamic Arab societies. As these societies are based on the principles of Western philosophy, and non-Muslim religious thought, instead of the belief in the sovereignty of Allah s.w.t., Qutb considers modern jahiliyya pervasive and complete. Jahiliyya forms the core of Qutb's revivalist zealotry and Qutb has been called "the exponent of jahiliyya par excellence (Kepel 1986:46; Choueiri 1990:123)

Qutb delineated his concept of jahiliyya in his most popular work Milestones, (*Maalim fi al-tariq, 1964: a substitute translation of the title is 'Signposts'*), a work that has inspired some of the most extreme expression of Islamic zealotry and puritanism. In "*Milestones,*" Qutb (1980 edn: 7-15, 286) argues:

"Mankind today is on the brink of a precipice, not because of the danger of complete annihilation which is hanging over its head – this being just a symptom and not the real disease – but because humanity is devoid of those vital values that are necessary not only for its healthy development but also for its real progress. Even the western world realizes that Western civilization is unable to present any healthy values for guidance of mankind. It knows that it does not possess anything which will satisfy its own conscience and justify its existence....It is essential for mankind to have a new leadership...It is necessary for the new leadership to preserve and develop the material fruits of the creative genius of Europe, and also to provide mankind with high ideals and values as have so far remained undiscovered by mankind, and which will also acquaint humanity with a way of life which is harmonious with human nature, which is positive and constructive, and which is practicable. Islam is the only system, which possesses these values and this way of life. If we look at the sources and foundations of modern way of living, it becomes clear that the whole world is steeped in jahiliyya (pagan ignorance of divine guidance), and not all the marvelous material comforts and high-level inventions diminish this ignorance."

Sayyid Qutb engaged his intransigent doctrine of Islam in a multi-dimensional jihad to overcome jahiliyya that called for violent resistance. He sought a restoration of the ideal Islamic identity and society which, he argued, required a "vanguard of the Ummah" that inspired by modeling communities on the original Qur'anic generation, "sweep away the influence of jahiliyya from our souls" and withdraw from the unbelieving, godless *dunya* (world) as a first step in replicating the communities of Muhammad's Ummah and the rightly guided caliphs.

Qutb believed that they were the proper model for the vanguard that would overcome jahiliyya and restore Allah's Quranic covenant. He insisted that interfaith dialogue and comprise with non-Muslims is impossible between the world of jahiliyya and the world of Islam: *"Islam, then, is the only Divine way of life which brings out the noblest human belief characteristics, developing and using them for a human society. Islam has remained unique in this respect to this day. Those who deviate from this system.... are truly enemies of mankind."* (Qutb, Milestones, III, 51) All who "deviate" from Islam, defined by Qutb and his Salafist zealots as the entire non-Muslim world, are without exception "truly enemies of mankind." He warns Muslims have therefore no choice but to take -up jihad against the post-modern culture of jahiliyya.

Qutb warns against the "naïve" assumption that da'wa ("preaching and exposition") can transform "the whole of humankind throughout the earth" to open their hearts to Islam. (Qutb, Milestones, IV, 63.) While he is not denying that *da'wa* has a role to play, Qutb disputes that the jahili world will place obstacles in the way and that committed Muslims must be compelled to remove them "by force."

Qutb's idea of jihad is consistent with the zealotry of Abu'l-A`la Mawdudi, and Muhammad ibn `Abd al-Wahhab the intellectual forefather of radical ideological Islam. Qutb disputes only true Muslim believers partake of full humanity while unbelievers are in some sense sub-human, apart from the human condition.

According to the abhorrent ideology of Qutb, the destruction of infidels violates no ethical or moral principle. Destroying unbelievers, however effected would be for the "Vanguard" a momentous occasion for the restoration of the world to an extremist conformity with what Qutb's views as pure Qur'anic thought.

In Qutb's theological aberration, violence and liquidation of unbelievers rests upon the mistaken conviction that mortal life is to be intrinsically naturally valued. In reality, Qutb and his zealous "Vanguard" argued that respect for life and fear of death are expressions of jahiliyya. His abhorrent interpretation of Islam contains all elements necessary to justify any kind of mass murder in the name of 'faith. It is significant to realize that Qutb did his writing from within the confines of an Egyptian prison. He saw himself more as a prophet, not as a strategist.

So who precisely does Wahhabism and its theological "vanguard" ISIL D'aesh threaten? It could not be clearer. It does not directly threaten Europe and the Americas (though westerners should remain wary, and not tread on this particular snake). The Saudi Ikhwani history is a clear and concise pollution to Islam.

As Ibn Saud and Abd al-Wahhab polluted Islam with aberrant zealotry the 18th century; and as the Saudi Ikhwan made it such in the 20th century. ISIL D'aesh's real target must be the Hijaz, the seizure of Mecca and Medina, and the legitimacy that this will confer on ISIL as the new Emirs of Arabia.

Islamic sunnah teaches that the sufferings, hunger, or evildoing of one member of the community is felt by all others. Therefore, the whole *Ummah* (community) is responsible for resolving each issue together. Together we must respond to the zealotry of Wahhabist and Salafist violent intolerance with *ijtihad* and qiyās, and become models of human compassion and peace, far outside the toxic shadows of ideology.

V. Hashishiyya and Nusa'iri: Shadows of Syria and Afghanistan

Sufi mystic poets in their verses show us that no religion has a monopoly over truth. That Sufism is the antique faith offering the relief of human misery and spiritual evanescence. For a Sufi, the World of Souls, and Light is the point where life starts and where it ends. Tracing its earliest theology to the lifetime of Muḥammad, the mystic sect of *Nizari Ismā'īlism* rose to become the most influential branch of Shī'ism, climaxing as a political power with the Fatimid Caliphate in the tenth through twelfth centuries. Nizari Ismā'īlīyya get their name from their acceptance of *Ismā'īl ibn Ja'far* as appointed spiritual successor, *Imām*, to *Ja'far aṣ-Ṣādiq*, herein they differ from the Twelvers, who distinguish *Mūsà al-Kāżim*, younger brother of *Ismā'īl*, as true Imām.

Hassan Ibn Sabbāh was a Persian mystic raised as a missionary and took his early education in Qumm, Persia. At the age of 17, Hassan converted to Nizari Ismā'īlism and swore allegiance to the Fatimid Caliphate in Cairo, Egypt. He continued his studies there for three years then traveled to Palestine, Syria, Azerbaijan, and Turkey after becoming a full missionary, or *Dā'ī*. Hassan's search for a base from where to guide his mission ended when he located the castle of Alamut (Arabic; *Aluh Amut* "Eagle's teaching") in the Rudbar area of northern Persia in 1088.

In the summer of 1090[AD], Hasan set out from Qazvin to Alamut on a mountainous route through Andej. He remained at Andej disguised as a schoolteacher named *Dikhhuda* until he was certain that a number of his supporters had strategically positioned below the castle in the village of Gazorkhan and had gained paid labor as scribes and tutors at the fortress itself.

During the early weeks of the month Rajab of Year 483 of the Islamic Hijri calendar, Sabbāh and around 30-40 of his loyal *hashishi* declared complete control of the fortress Alamut. Historians record that Sabbāh's band of hashishi swore their lives to his new teaching on the 14th day of Rajab establishing the first oaths of the *Hashishiyya*. (Virani, Shafique N. *"Ismailis in the Middle Ages: A*

History of Survival, A Search for Salvation" (New York: Oxford University Press, 2007), 29.)

It was September 11, 1090.

    Hassan's takeover of the fort was one of silent surrender in the face of defeated odds. To affect this takeover Hassan employed an ingenious strategy: it took the better part of two years to effect. First Hassan sent his *Da'iyyīn* and *Rafīks* (missionaries and foot soldiers) to entice the villages in the valley over through propaganda. Next, key Ulema were converted and by the end of 1090, Hassan took over the fort, establishing a base for his theology and political exploits. Hasan bin Sabbāh compiled a theological treatise in this context, entitled *Fusul-i Arba'a*, "The Four Chapters," which was an *Ismā'īli* thesis, and the doctrine of *talim* was expounded by him in this Persian tract.

    The *Hashishi* of the *Nizari Ismā'īliyya* sect caught the attention of Crusaders and Medieval historians with the increase in their political assassinations. Medieval historians designated the Hashishi pejoratively as *Batiniyya* (esotericists, or sorcerers), or *Ta'limiyya*, sometimes Nizāriyyah. Hashishi, like all *Nizari Ismā'īliyya* were designated *malahida*, or *mulhiddun*; derogatory terms meaning "heretics."

    The terms *al-Hashishiyya* (the hashish users), and *Jama'at al-Hashishiyya* (community of the hashish takers) were meant to be abusive and belittling by anti-Nizari polemical edicts, or fatwas, issued by the Fatimid chancery around 1123[A.D.] on behalf of the Caliph. This anti-Nizari condemnation of *Hashishiyya* stemmed from Sunni theological disapproval and the growing political crisis of the First Crusades.

    These abusive terms first applied to the Syrian Hashishi in the early decades of the twelfth century, indicating a general familiarity with the sect in Syria and Egypt. Many of the terms were used interchangeably by orthodox Sunni Imams. Hashishi is not used by Persian historians Rashid al-Din, and Juwayni of the Nizari period, who are the main sources of information on the sect in the Fatimid Caliphate. Muslim historian Ibn Khaldūn uses the term *Fidawiyya* (zealots), in reference to al-Hashishi writing after the thirteenth century. Based on historical references the Hashishi were rarely referred to as "hashishi takers" until decades after Hasan bin Sabbāh.

Hashish use in Syria, Egypt, and Persia grew extensively by lower social strata. Muslim scholars wrote numerous tracts on the effects of hashish use in various physical, mental, ethical, and religious considerations. Hashish users were commonly considered social outcasts and religious heretics.

The few Islamic historians that refer to the Nizaris as Hashishiyya, like Juwayni, never explain the reasons for this label in terms of hashish use, though heaping libelous accusations upon the sect that enabled exotic fantasies by Medieval European historians such as Marco Polo.

The *Nusa'iri* are an ostensibly Shi'a Muslim society living in the eponymous Al'Ansariyah mountain range along the Mediterranean coast in northwestern Assyria. Presently, Nusa'iri reside in all cities of Syria, estimated to account for twenty-percent of the Syrian populace, about three million. Expeditionary travelers and historians have mistaken the Nusa'iri for the Isma'ili and Druze; both sects have fought with the neighboring Nusa'iri for over a thousand years.

The Druze are an esoteric monotheistic religious community living in Syria, Lebanon, Israel, and Jordan, emerging during the 11th century from Nizari Ismāʿīlism and incorporated ritual elements of Gnosticism, Neo-Platonism and Shamanistic drug usage. The Druze call themselves Ahl al' Tawhid; "those who affirm the unity of God," or al'Muwaḥḥidūn "Unitarians."

We must note, that like all mystic sects including the *Nizari Isma'ili Hashishiyya* {Order of the Hashish takers, or Assassins}, the Nusa'iri are notorious not for their actual verifiable history, but more for the information given by their accusers and political enemies {Druzes}. Frater Randolph in this manner likely encountered information, realizing the Nusa'iri were the subject of extensive persecution under Shi'a, Druze, and Christian Crusaders. Randolph undoubtedly encountered their priesthood in his Arabian travels, setting their sexual rites of antiquity aside from Gnosticism and Neo-Platonism of the Druze, Zoroastrians, Yezidi, and Mandaeans.

Western society first learned of these ostensive Muslims through the logs of explorers Carsten Niebuhr and C.F. Volney from 1783-1785. Volney was an anthropologist who discussed the Nusa'iri at length in his published work *Voyage en Egypte et en Syrie* (1787). A contemporary of Voltaire's philosophy, Comte de Volney had a dystopian opinion of the human condition, and believed the bizarre tales he had heard of Nusa'iri ritual erotica as probable while Niebuhr, a more utilitarian perceiver, believed no group could be so depraved.

In his *Voyage en Egypte et en Syrie*, Volney reports a variety of belief in Nusa'iri practice, such as metempsychosis, some refuting the soul's perceivability or theosis, sacred prostitution, and veneration of the sex organs {*qadmousié*}, a theme which reappears in the tracts of Nusa'iri's enemies and in later Islamic, and historical literature.

The *Qadmousié* were believed to assemble for nocturnal rites, consecrate participants with myrrh and rose oils and various bodily fluids, ingest hashish, and engage in indiscriminate sex, as Volney claimed "like ancient Gnostics" yet he admitted never attending any Nusa'iri ritual saturnalia, restricted to Nusa'iri initiates alone.

The next tract on the *Nusa'iri*, *Exposé de la Religion des Druses* (1838), written by Orientalist Baron Antoine-Sylvestre de Sacy reports a diatribe from the Druze sect, and their prophet, Hamza ibn'Alī ibn Aḥmad. Hamza's vehemence toward the Nusa'iri is well established by scholars and we can more than speculate that his reports stem from political and religious diatribes against the Nusa'iri. Hamza does state he 'discovered' a tome received from a Nusa'iri that was so obscene he had to refute it.

The tomes of the Druze and Nusa'iri were so theologically syncretic because sexual imagery was used by both sects rather than metaphoric interpretation, leading to the confusion were various charges of moral depravity. Hamza stated that according to the Nusa'iri, metempsychosis was enabled only through secret sex ceremonies. De Sacy likened the sex magic of the Nusa'iri to the Hashashin ritual usage of hashish to artificially create the paradise of the "Old Man of the Mountain," Hassan ibn Sabbāh.

Next in the sequence of Nusa'iri historians who provide second-hand accounts of their assemblage, is French poet Gérard de Nerval theorizing that the Nusa'iri and Druze were responsible for the occult revival of the nineteenth century. Nerval theorized that the Nusa'iri influenced the Knights Templar, as told to him by the son of an English attaché in Tripoli who allegedly wedded a Nusa'iri woman and learned much of their nocturnal assemblies.

Nerval reports second-handedly from his source that Nusa'iri priests prostrated themselves before a nude sacred prostitute on an altar and before every female, they encountered in daily activity, also at the rising of Venus each year the Nusa'iri initiates congregated into a domed chapel, extinguished the lights, and engaged in indiscriminate debauch.

Shi'a Muslim controversy in the twelfth century theorized perhaps in an act of intentional deception to rival Druze, or Sunni sects, associated Nusa'iri with '*nasrani*,' vestiges of an ethno-religious group from Kerala, India, adhering to the church of the Saint Thomas Christian tradition. They are also known as Syrian-Malabar Christians, *Suriyani Christiaanikal, Mar Thoma Nasrani*, or more popularly as Syrian Christians in view that they use Syriac liturgy.

The Nusa'iri's themselves considered this name derogatory and prefer the name, *Alawi* to the latter recognizing their association with 'Ali ibn Abi Talib, rather than Abu Shu'ayb Muhammad Ibn Nusayr. {Abd 'Allah, Umar F., *Islamic Struggle in Syria*, Berkeley: Mizan Press, c1983, p.43-48}

Rosicrucian Adept, and Beverly Pascal Randolph's successor, R. Swinburne Clymer in his print journal, *Initiates and the People Part 2, May 1929 to June 1930* refers to the Nusa'iri as the ancient Ansari, the converts of Prophet Muhammad s.a.w., during the Flight to

Medina. In the 19th and 20th centuries, however, an Alawite named Sulaiman al'Adni converted to Christianity and compiled a book called *Al'Bakurah as'Suliamaniya fi Kashf Asrar ad'Diyanah an'Nusairiyah* {*The First Fruits of Sulaiman in Revealing the Secrets of the Nusairi Religion*} in 1863. Orientalist Louis Massignon gained access to a number of Nusairi manuscripts and provided a less biased and ill-informed account than Nerval and de Sacy.

Much of the Nusa'iri, or Alawi, and Druze genealogies was inconclusive guesswork under a myriad guise of mythos and phallic symbolism. Worship of the generative energies connects with a mystic mythology of the ancients. Occultists and historians have fascinated themselves with mystic theologies of Arabia and the Fertile Crescent, where secret brotherhoods such as the Hashashin, Druze, and Nusa'iri who they believed retained centuries-old secrets of elixirs and sex magic.

According to scholar, Massignon, Alawis have integrated doctrines from other esoteric Islamic societies, in particular from Isma'ilis, Bardesanian, and Valentinian Gnosticism. It is theorized that "as a small, historically beleaguered ethnic group", the Alawi 'absorbed elements' from the different religions that influenced their area from Hellenistic times onward, while maintaining their own beliefs, and pretended to adhere to the dominant religion of the age." {Abd-Allah, Umar F., *Islamic Struggle in Syria*, Berkeley: Mizan Press, c1983, p.43-48}

'Abd-Allah theorizes that the Alawis and Isma'ilis believed Islamic Shari'a had esoteric, allegorical, *Batini* meaning and an exoteric, literal, *zahiri* meaning and that only the hidden meaning is intended. Alawis believe the esoteric meaning is known only to their Imams. A volume on the Nusa'iri that has withstood the test of scholarship since Randolph's publishing of the Anseiratic Mysteries is a summary that appeared in the Journal of American Oriental Society in 1866. The volume is a purported confession of a Nusa'iri exile from their community translated by Christian missionaries in Beirut, Lebanon.

The Alawi secrets are only revealed in initiatic progression to adult members of the community. Alawis believed in a triune manifestation or schema in the divine, `Ain-Mim-Sin, which represents `Ali, *Muhammad*, the divine Communicator, and *Salman al'Farsi*, the Persian Companion of the expressed deity, Muhammad.

Alawi initiates were taught that the soul originated as emanations of sentient light down through vast hierarchies of orders and angels to humans. Human beings were fundamentally particles of light, originally wandering stars yet now trapped in physical human incarnations. The particles of light fell in their belief that they were equal to `Ali, falling into particles of matter in space-time continuums and then into human sexual differentiation.

Alawi initiates aspired to release their souls from cyclic successions of transfiguration, by recognizing `Ali. Muhammad manifested his incarnation, known as *ism*, or "name," `Ali as *bab*, or 'door,' and Salman al'Farsi as *ma'na*, or 'meaning,' the esoteric lineage of Nusa'iri origination. Muhammad and `Ali were believed to be emanations of Salman al'Farsi. According to Abd-Allah, each of these three is said to have been an incarnation of Al'lah.

To Alawi initiates, `Ali, constitutes the most important part of the triune. The Alawi testimony of faith is: *"I have borne witness that there is no God but He, the most High, the object of worship al `Ali al'Ma'bud and that there is no concealing veil (hijab) except the lord Muhammad, the object of praise, (as 'Sayyid Muhammad al-Mahmud), and there is not Bab except the lord Salman al'Farisi`."*

Beginning in the 1820's, a group of *da 'is* (missionaries) were appointed by a combined movement of Oxford University, the Anglican Church, and Kings College of London University, under the Ancient & Accepted Scottish Rite; the collusion fostered the creation of an occult brotherhood in the Muslim world, dedicated to the use of terrorism on behalf of the Freemasons and Order of the Garter in the City of London.

The leading promoters of the Oxford Movement were Prime Minister Benjamin Disraeli, Lord Palmerstone of the Palladian Rite, and Frater Edward Bulwer-Lytton, the leader of a branch of Rosicrucianism that developed from the Asiatic Brethren, or the *Fratres Lucis*. Benjamin Disraeli was Grand Master of Freemasonry, as well as knight of the Order of the Garter.

Bulwer-Lytton was the Grand Patron of the *Societas Rosicruciana in Anglia* (SRIA), founded in 1865 by Frater Robert Wentworth Little, and based on the rituals of Fratres Lucis, had become members of a German Masonic lodge called *L'Aurore Naissante*, or "the Nascent Dawn", founded in Frankfurt-on-Main in 1807. It was at *L'Aurore Naissante* where Lord Bulwer Lytton initiated. In Egypt, the Oxford movement centered on the *Salafists*, to serve the Brotherhoods in protecting their trade by the Suez Canal, crucial to the shipment of their oil cargo to Europe and British Colonial India.

Jamaluddin al'Afghani enrolled in a madrasah in the holy city of Najaf, in Iraq. There, Afghani initiated into the Babist mysteries of Sheikh ibn Zayn ibn Ibráhím al'Ahsá'í. Ahsá'í was succeeded after his death by Sayyid Kāẓim bin Qāsim al'Ḥusaynī Rashtī, who introduced the idea of a 'perfect Shi'ah,' in Islam called *Bab*, meaning "gate," who is to come.

An initiate of the Babist mysteries, Mírzá Ḥusayn`Alí Núrí, declared himself the emanation of the "One greater than Himself," predicted by the Bab (Sayyid Rashtī), assuming the title of Bahá'u'lláh, Arabic for "Glory of God." In 1866, Jamaluddin al 'Afghani became confidential counselor to Azam, the Sultan in Afghanistan.

In 1871, Afghani went to Cairo, sponsored by Prime Minister Mustafa Pasha, acquainted with him in Istanbul, and then placed him salary, with a prestigious tenure at the university of Al'Azhar. Afghani's theology remained strictly orthodox Shi'a, yet in 1878, he relocated to Cairo's old Jewish quarter, where he announced the formation of the Arab Masonic Society.

Afghani became an initiate of the Hermetic Brotherhood of Luxor in Cairo, Egypt, or the Sabian teachings of the Grand Lodge of the of Cairo Ismāʿīliyya; a fraternal society dedicated to Masonry, philosophy, and Nizari Ismāʿīliyya. In Cairo, Afghani studied with two initiates in the Hermetic Brotherhood of Luxor; James Sanua, and Lydia Pashkov. Sanua and Lydia Pashkov were companions of Helena Petrovna Blavatsky, A Russian mystic who founded the Theosophical Society in 1875.

Through her sacred studies and acquaintance with Jamaluddin al'Afghani, Blavatsky assimilated her doctrines of theosophy, derived from Ismāʿīlism, which she would disseminate to the Invisible College of the Western Mystery Schools. Unknown to scholars, Blavatsky cites Afghani anonymously in her tomes, *Isis Unveiled* and *The Secret Doctrine*. She claims to have received these works from a "Persian Sufi," as scholar K. Paul Johnson points out, Afghani is the likely reference.

According to Johnson, a fundamental structure in Blavatsky's theosophy originates from one source; Ismāʿīlism. *The Chaldean Book of Numbers* professes a sevenfold cosmology similar to Nizari Ismāʿīliyya. "The centrality of the number seven," notes Johnson:
" *...is a major clue which points to Ismaili gnosis as an important source for both Blavatsky and Gurdjieff. Henri Corbin's Cyclical Time and Ismaili Gnosis describes the doctrine of a sevenfold cosmic evolutionary process, repeated in a sevenfold historical scheme, paralleled by a sevenfold initiatory path for the individual adept. This corresponds exactly to the Mahatma letters [of Blavatsky] teaching that "the degrees of an Adept's initiation mark the seven stages at which he discovers the secret of the sevenfold principles in nature and man and awakens his dormant powers." The doctrine of the Resurrection acquires a specific meaning in Ismaili gnosis, which relates it to Blavatsky's teachings. Each of the seven principles of the individual is "resurrected" by the influence of the next higher principle. HPB's sevenfold breakdown of human principles was presented variously as Chaldean, Tibetan, and Chaldeo-Tibetan. But in fact its closest historical analogue is Ismaili."* [The Masters Revealed, pp. 146]

Paschal Beverly Randolph thrust himself into this labyrinth when announcing his intention to publish the secret of the Ansaireh (*Nusaʾiriyya*, a mystical sect of Muslims in Syria known today as the Alawis) priesthood in *The New Mola* (1873). In *Eulis*, he writes of his encounter with a Nusa'iri maiden: "*One night – it was in far-off Jerusalem or Bethlehem, I really forget which, – I made love to, and was loved by, a dusky maiden of Arabic blood. I of her, and that experience, learned – not directly, but by suggestion – fundamental principle of the White Magic of Love; subsequently I became affiliated with some dervishes and fakirs of whom, by suggestion, still, I found the road to other knowledges; and of these devout practicers of a simple, but sublime and holy magic, I obtained additional clues – little threads of suggestion, which, persistently followed, led my soul into labyrinths of knowledge themselves did not even suspect the existence of. I became practically, what I was naturally – a mystic, and in time chief of the lofty brethren; taking the clues left by the masters, and pursuing them farther than they had ever been before; actually discovering the ELIXIR OF LIFE; the universal Solvent, or celestial Alkahest; the water of beauty and perpetual youth, and the philosopher's stone.*"

In 1873, Carl Kellner, a fraternal associate of Brother Randolph, was another of the many occultists associated with Egyptian Freemasonry, traveling to Cairo in the time of Afghani's activity. There he met, for the first time, a Luxor initiate by the name of Brother Aya Aziz, also known as Max Théon. Théon was the son of the last leader of the Frankist sect, Rabbi Judes Lion Bimstein of Warsaw, Poland.

In Cairo, Théon worked with Blavatsky, and became a student of Paulos Metamon, a Coptic Initiate. Paulos Metamon was also Blavatsky's first tutor, whom she had met in Asia Minor in 1848, and again in Cairo in 1870, as Metamon introduced her to the Hermetic Brotherhood of Light, the Fratres Lucis, and a continuation of the Asiatic Brethren.

Afghani's departed Egypt to Afghanistan, while his pupil, Mohammed Abduh, was inexplicably named the chief editor of the official British colonial press of the Egyptian government, the Journal Official. Working under him was a Freemason, Sa'ad Zaghul, founder of the Wafd nationalist party. Abduh traveled throughout the Arab world, under various names, particularly to Tunis, Beirut, and Damascus, Syria.

In each city he journeyed, Abduh initiated members into the secret society of Afghani's Salafi fundamentalism. The secret Salafi movement then became allied with the Wahhabis of Saudi Arabia, through the doctrines of another Arab Freemason, Mohammed Rashid Rida. After the death of Afghani in 1897, and Abduh in 1905, Rida assumed the leadership of the Salafi secret society, changing the course of history in Egypt, and the Kingdom of Saud; ideological currents still affecting the world stage from the shadows in the 21st century.

VI. Roshaniyya: the Illuminated Ones of Afghanistan

Bayazid al 'Ansari {1525-1581} was born poverty-stricken into the Arab tribe of Madinah, mentioned in the Holy Qu'ran, which received the Prophet Muhammad after his flight from Makkah {Mecca}. The name Ansari is an offshoot of the Madinah tribe and derives from the Arabic, al'ansar, meaning "assistants," or "helpers."

The al'ansar were the historical saintly individuals of the Madinah tribe whom assisted and gave refuge to the Prophet Muhammad who fled Makkah in self-exile from the Persian Manichaean and Zoroastrian chieftains. Islamic Scholar Idries Shah Naqshbandi contends that the given birth name of al 'Ansari was Fateh Bayazid Khan, the son of a Sufi Mullah from the family of Bayazid, in the Madinah tribe of Afghanistan and Pakistan.

During the life of Bayazid Al'Ansari Afghanistan and Pakistan were governed as independent provinces often contested by the Persian Safavid Empire and the Mughal Empire in India, of the Sixteenth and Seventeenth Centuries A.D. Raised in the humble and poor backgrounds of Sufi khanikahs {residential communities}, Bayazid al 'Ansari was not born into the Pashtun tribe, yet his maternal lineage linked his family to the Pashtuns, a tribe of modern day Afghanistan. Shah indicates that al 'Ansari possibly grew up a neglected or abused child, likely common in the war torn provinces of Kandahar, Herat, and Kabul before the Mughals brought Islamic renaissance in Art, literature, music, and economics to the region.

Although there is no known historical-magical record of al 'Ansari initiating into a Sufi tariqat, {order} he is known to have diligently studied Sufi practices of *dhikr* {remembrance of Allah, s.w.t.}, *qilwat* {concentration}, and *tawhid* {unity}. Al'ansar eventually claimed some degree of illumination thereby, perhaps attaining *ahadiyyat* {oneness} or his sirr, divine genius in the practice of tasawwuf, Sufism. Traveling to north of Peshawar, al 'Ansari inaugurated and opened up a modest khanikahs {residential school}. The Sufi devotee commenced training a small body of Aspirants in the supernatural and mystical sciences he acquired; he taught that the

Supreme Being, the First Cause, Allah the Benevolent and Merciful, desired the creation of a new class of Illuminated Men and Women to govern the world.

Aspirants were placed in a carefully supervised vigil of seclusion and meditation {qilwat}. The now zealous and illuminated neophytes turned their loved ones and patrons onto this new system, soon Ansari was lavishly provided for by wealthy merchants and Pashtun tribal Chieftains. Al'Ansari began to prosper in wealth.

Through his increasing works and popularity among local aspirants, al 'Ansari became known as the *Pir'i'Roshan*, or the "Apostle of Light" by his beloved devotees. The collected writings of al 'Ansari, "*Khayr al-Bayan*," "*Maksud al-Muminin*" "*Surat-i Tawhid*," "*Fakr*," and "*Hal-Nama*" formed the basis of a movement referred to as the Roshaniyya by followers and critics of al 'Ansari alike.

The fledgling movement rapidly flourished in the region of Kabul, spreading in popularity and sensationalism into areas of Mughal Kashmir. The Sunni Ulema vigorously opposed the Sufi philosophy and writings of al 'Ansari's Roshaniyya sect.

In the mid-Sixteenth century, Mughal governors increased persecution of his followers and executed many of them in the name of orthopraxy in Islam. Scholar Idries Shah offers that Isma'ili missionaries had direct association with the Roshaniyya sect. Nonetheless, Bayazid Ansari seems to have been influenced with the esoteric doctrines of the Nizari Ismailites in Kandahar.

Many a bulk of the Isma'ili tés were also scourged to death in Kashmir during the Mughal operations, forcing the surviving members of the sect to migrate to Punjab, where they emerged under the name of the Shamsi. The Nizari Isma'ili tés are best known for the radical sect of Hashishiyya, or Assassins founded by Hasan ibn Sabbāh in A.D. 1090.

Bayazid al 'Ansari instituted the foundations of the Roshaniyya sect in A.D. 1542-1543 the period when the majority of the aforementioned writings were collectively published. His religious teachings spread rapidly amongst the Pashtun. Eventually, at length, al 'Ansari gained the ability to assemble Roshaniyya militias, and oppose the Mughal government. Al 'Ansari was a zealous adherent of Sufi mystical practices. Idries Shah attributes his discipleship under the notorious Mullah Sulayman {known as Jalandhari Sulayman, from the town of Jalandhar, in Panjab} to increased attention from the Mughal government.

Under Mullah Sulayman, al 'Ansari initiated in the tenets of the Raja Yogis, a practice among Hindu sects, and became a fast convert to the creed of the Metempsychosis, a Pythagorean system of the transmigration of souls. On these doctrines, however, he engrafted some of his own personal Sufi mystical practices, the most remarkable of which was, that the most complete manifestations of Allah s.w.t., were attained in the persons of the enlightened, or "illuminated." The great opponent of Bayazid al 'Ansari was Akhund Darwazah, the greatest and most venerated of all the saints of Afghanistan, whom in derision of the title of Pir'i'Roshan, conferred with his initiating Mullah upon al 'Ansari the name of Pir'i 'Tarik, or "Apostle of Darkness," by which name he is now chiefly known.

Bayazid al 'Ansari strategic association with particular influential Pashtun P{Pathan} tribal chieftains, in addition to ostracizing himself outside of the tribal system, segregating himself independent of a single tribal patronage, al 'Ansari was able to meld an identity greater than the tribal level. He molded the sect of the Roshaniyya in the rustic mountains of Afghanistan, formulating Eight degrees of Initiation similar to the initiatic grades of the Sufi tariqas {religious orders}, thus inaugurating a greater sense of identity; a greater Islamic identity and an identity as a Roshaniyya.

Thus were given the Roshaniyya a keen edge by the anti-Mughal political maneuverings of al 'Ansari. However, his opponent Darwaza's connection to knowledgeable and established elders whom were well steeped not only in the formal sciences of Islam, but also were highly familiar with the mystical traditions of the Sufi tariqas.

Darwazah also was initiated in light exercises that form the foundations of the ascent through the planes to the Sufi Mevlevi Dervish, initiated into the magical language and allusions by which religion is transmitted. This knowledge unfortunately offset the strategic edge of the Roshaniyya. In fact, it was a teacher of Darwazah, a scholar by the name of Mullah Zangi Pabini, whom actually first mentioned conferring upon al 'Ansari the dubious title of Pir'i' Tarik.

The Roshaniyya sect were fervently opposed by the Sunni Ulema and more orthodox Sufis alike, as well as the Mughals government under Shah Akbar {1556-1605}. With partial sovereignty over regional provinces of Peshawar, Kabul, Heart, and Kandahar in modern Afghanistan and Kashmir, the Mughal government vigorously initiated military and subversive campaigns against the Roshaniyya. Many Roshaniyya were arrested and executed by the Mughals.

These events became the first broad scale religious and political movement uniting the then divided Afghan, Pashtun speaking, tribes of the region. The Roshaniyya movement lingered on until the Eighteenth Century when the last Roshaniyya initiate purportedly died in $^{A.D.}$ 1736; nonetheless, the movement profoundly affected Afghan culture.

Modern Isma'ili scholars Farhad Daftary, Bernard Lewis, and Idries Shah theorize that Isma'ili missionaries had known albeit shadowed relations with the Roshaniyya sect, as the esoteric doctrines of Shaykh Bayazid al 'Ansari are marked with influences of the esoteric doctrines prevalent of the Nizari Isma'ilis in Kandahar.

A bulk number of Kashmiri Isma'ilis were killed in reprisals from the Mughal army during Mughal campaigns in the region. Such points to a closer connection between the Nizari Isma'ili sect of the Hashishiyya and Shaykh Bayazid al 'Ansari's Roshaniyya as scholars ambiguously suggest. Bayazid al 'Ansari died in $^{A.D.}$ 1581 from wounds received in the Battle of Dawlatabad.

Franz Kolmer, a Danish merchant had made innumerable trips to Egypt and Persia, living for several years in Alexandria, Egypt. The elusive Franz Kolmer was a Freemason of good standing in the German Grand Lodge, and as the tale is circulated, heard of the Roshaniyya during his studies in Alexandria and travels to Safavid Persia, as the last Roshaniyya initiate allegedly died in 1736. In 1770, Kolmer became acquainted with Jesuit Priest and Professor at Ingolstadt, Adam Weishaupt. On 1 May 1776, Weishaupt and Baron Adolph-François-Frederic Knigge along with Mayer Amschel Rothschild inaugurated the Bavarian Order of Perfectibilists, later known as the Bavarian Order of the Illuminati.

VII. Sufism, Freemasons, and the Illuminati

Sufism is revealed in the world by means of itself, while occultism in the United States and Europe is revealed by means of progressive initiations, yet in the 21st century there is no longer any such thing as "occultism" in the United States, or Europe. Surrounded by modes of digital exposure on a global scale, Sufism retains its mystic quality without theological dissemination.

Sufism is the grand demarcation between the human subconscious mind and religion. Where American occultism is concerned with the pursuit and collection of hidden teachings and the engineering of consciousness, Sufism's concern is for the freedom of ideas, intolerance against cruelty, hypocrisy, and religious persecution; their opposition was to injustice and political crime. Their stories were the subject of divine intoxication, love, and human suffering.

Sufism is the biography of humanity, *ṣalawāt* and *dhikr* are the zakāt of time. Their poetry and writings defy fortune and wealth, outliving the world's calamities. They are an eternal edifice surviving all empires, conquerors, kings, and revolutions. Sufism is a comfort to the broken heart, immortalizing the poet, consoling the mind's silent tragedies. These courageous souls paint visions of apocalypse and ecstasy across history and human arts.

Sufism is the Arabic parent of the Western Mystery Tradition, the true "Eastern Star" of the Western Mystery Schools. The Arabic word for Mason, is *al'Banna*, "builder." The fundamental word for the Royal Arch School of Masonry is *Jahbulon*, composed usually of the Hebrew letters, Aleph, Beth, and Lamed – A, B, and L. According to The Rev. Canon Richard Tydeman, in an address to the Supreme Grand Chapter of England on 13 November 1985, the word is a compound of three Hebrew terms: יה *Jah*, I AM, which indicates eternal existence, בעל B'El, on high, in heaven) and און *On*, strength; pronouncing three aspects or qualities of Deity, namely Eternal Existence, Transcendence, and Omnipotence and equating to The True and Living God.

According to Stephen Knight, following Walton Hannah, the word is a compound of the names of three gods worshipped in the ancient Middle East: Yahweh/Ja, Baal, and On, a name in Genesis in the Bible in Potiphar priest of On; thought in older times to be a name of Osiris. The letters A, B, and L represent the Sufi watchword *al'Banna*. To the Sufi builders, the word intimates initiation and the three letters symbolize key meditation postures. A, *alif*, is the kneeling posture. The second letter, B, *ba*, is symbolic of prostration and concentration. The third letter, L, *lam* in Arabic is shaped like a rope. To the builder, lam means 'the rope which binds all in mediation.'

The letters *alif*, *ba*, and *lam* according to the mystic Abjad table when added together produce the sum of 33. *Alif* ا = 1, *ba* ب = 2, and *lam* 30 = ل. According to the Sufi builders, this code is an intimation of the letter Q, the Masonic letter 'G,' inscribed by the builders with a pentagram. The lower triangle correlates to the shaped Arabic numeral seven, the upper is the outline of the numeral eight, with the sides of the triangles comprising the sum of six. The series 786 is the esoteric code of *Bismillah ar-Rahman ar-Rahim* reduced by direct substitution in the Abjad. The phrase means In the name of *Allah the Beneficent, the Merciful.*

Surah 24 *An-Nur* of the Qur'an illuminates the heart of Sufi mysticism. The verse *An-Nur* means "The Light," expounds on the nature of *nur*, with Essence/Being, *wujud* the evanescence of the dimensions of human consciousness outside of intellect and emotion. *Nur* can never be truly seen and nothing may encompass it, contrasted with Darkness, *zulma*, Nothingness, as the cosmos is seen as an emanation of light between the *Allah* and *Zulma*. Surah 24 *An-Nur* teaches that our Eternal Position in the Divine Presence is in the World of Souls and Light.

Compare Surah 24 (verse 35) *An-Nur*: *"ALLAH is the reflection the Light to the heavens and earth. His Light resembles a lamp within a niche. The lamp is enclosed in a crystal, like a brilliant star. Lit from a blessed tree, an olive, not of the East or the West; of it the oil is well nigh-luminous, though the sacred fire touches it, Light upon Light!"* and Surah 86 *El Tariq*, (verse 1-4) the Night

Visitant: *"In the name of God, most benevolent, ever-merciful…How will you comprehend what the night star is? It is the star that shines with a piercing brightness… That over each soul there is a guardian."* Nature and life are a conundrum; we are here to make out the mysteries of life and death and draw them into the Light. Sufi mystics are the guardians of secret teachings of all ages obscured by an underculture of living shadows determined to find the antique faith in plain sight.

Qutub in Sufi terminology refer to the reputed invisible heads of all Sufis, of all Sufi tariqas and lineal chains. The word means, "pivot, chief, pole" transfigured to the sum 111 with the Abjad table. Qutbuddin are guides on earth who know the secret powers of the heart could reprogram their minds and psyche at will, and can unlock the underlying secrets of human psychology. Qutbuddin are the conquerors of hearts, the lords of annihilation represented by black robes frequently worn by dervishes and Sufi masters. Qutb in Sufism is the perfect human being, *al-insān al-kāmil*, a "pole" leading all Sufis and all men. There are said to be only five Qutbuddin living at once in any period of history.

The knowledge and possession of secret religious formulas is necessary for the station of *quṭubiyyah*, the mystic state of perfection of a Sufi Qutb. *Quṭubiyyah* correlates to the Christian mystic state of Gnosis, or saintly beatification. The transcendent reality taught by the Sufis and the Prophet Muhammad, Arabic – *al-ḥaqīqa al-muḥammadiyya* resembles the sun, and the hearts of the Qutbuddin are moons reflecting the permanent light of Allah. According to many Sufis, the elite stage of mysticism for Qutbuddin beings at the end of the point of spiritual prophet-hood. The end of the prophets therefore would be the starting point for the spiritual elite, the Qutbuddin, or "illuminated ones."

The *Qutb* is the axis or pivot and the highest station in the Sufi hierarchy. Qutbuddin are directly responsible for the welfare of the entire world. Qutbuddin are said to be the spiritual successor of Prophet Muhammad. All Sufis are in essence, reflections of Qutbuddin; they believe in the integrity of the human race. Sufis urge the existential self to attain an organic union with the human species and with the meta-physical ground of the cosmos. Sufis value life, personality, art, and transcendent love. Sufis do not claim their teachings as a religion or even a law of human social development. Sufism is an uprising, an intifada, and reinstatement of the human species' latent spiritual and intellectual impulses under the aegis of universal philosophy.

Sufi mystic poets in their verses show us that no religion has a monopoly over truth. That Sufism is the antique faith offering the relief of human misery and spiritual evanescence. For a Sufi, the World of Souls, and Light is the point where life starts and where it ends. Tracing its earliest theology to the lifetime of Muḥammad, the mystic sect of *Nizari Ismāʿīlism* rose to become the most influential branch of Shīʿism, climaxing as a political power with the Fatimid Caliphate in the tenth through twelfth centuries. Nizari Ismāʿīlīyya get their name from their acceptance of *Ismāʿīl ibn Jaʿfar* as appointed spiritual successor, *Imām*, to *Jaʿfar aṣ-Ṣādiq*, herein they differ from the Twelvers, who distinguish *Mūsà al-Kāẓim*, younger brother of *Ismāʿīl*, as true Imām.

The teachings of Sufism orchestrate throughout history within secret societies, traced in pedigree and language with syncretism. In the Twenty-first century, Christianity, Judaism, and Islam all share a fragile precarious world stage, leading societies teasingly close to economic and social ruin in the name of faith and "liberty and equality," the opiate of religions.

Consider that fundamentalist Muslims and paranoid conspiracy producers, determined to expose a "new world order," commonly tag the antique faith of Sufism. Sufi societies contribute and engage in humanitarian endowments of education, scholarship, chivalry, and public service for a greater good ignored by a cadre of conspiracy racketeers.

Orthodox Islam, both Sunni and Shi'a generally prohibit the practice of Freemasonry, and forbid Muslims to join Masonic Lodges in Arab nations with a Shari'ah legal system, An influential body interpreting Islamic Law correlating interfaith dialogue is the Islamic Jurisdictional College. At its meeting on 15 July 1978, it issued an opinion concerning *"The Freemasons' Organization."* The IJC declared: *"After complete research concerning this organization, based on written accounts from many sources, we have determined that:*
Freemasonry is a clandestine organization, which conceals or reveals its system, depending on the circumstances. Its actual principles are hidden from members, except for chosen members of its higher degrees.

The members of the organization, worldwide, are drawn from men without preference for their religion, faith, or sect.

The organization attracts members based on providing personal benefits. It traps men into being politically active, and its aims are unjust.

New members participate in ceremonies of different names and symbols, and are frightened from disobeying its regulations and orders.

Members are free to practice their religion, but only members who are atheists are promoted to its higher degrees, based on how much they are willing to serve its dangerous principles and plans.

It is a political organization. It has served all revolutions, military and political transformations. In all dangerous changes, a relation to this organization appears either exposed or veiled.

It is a Jewish Organization in its roots. Its secret higher international administrative board are Jews and it promotes Zionist activities.

Its primary objectives are the distraction of all religions and it distracts Muslims from Islam.

It tries to recruit influential financial, political, social, or scientific people to utilize them. It does not consider applicants it cannot utilize. It recruits kings, prime ministers, high government officials and similar individuals.

It has branches under different names as a camouflage, so people cannot trace its activities, especially if the name of "Freemasonry" has opposition. These hidden branches are known as Lions, Rotary and others. They have wicked principles that completely contradict the rules of Islam. There is a clear relationship between Freemasonry, Judaism, and International Zionism. It has controlled the activities of high Arab officials in the Palestinian problem. It has limited their duties, obligations, and activities for the benefit of Judaism and International Zionism."

The Society of the Muslim Brothers chartered in 1928 in Cairo, Egypt by the Islamic scholar and schoolteacher Sheikh Hasan Ahmed Abdel Rahman Muhammed al'Banna. When Hasan al'Banna was twelve years old, he became a student of the *Hasafiya Sufi order*, becoming a fully initiated member in 1922. Banna's father was as student of Abduh, and himself was greatly influenced by Rashid

Rida's Salafi fundamentalism. The Muslim Brotherhood originated as a religious social organization, tutoring the illiterate, establishing charitable hospitals and providing endowment for local enterprises. As the Brotherhood's social influence widened starting in 1936, it began stridently opposing British colonialism in Egypt.

In 1952 the Egyptian monarch King Farouk I was overthrown by nationalist military officers led by Colonel Gamel Abdel Nasser and General Muhammad Naguib supported by the Brotherhood. On 26 October, an assassination attempt was carried out against Nasser during a rally in Alexandria. The attempt to assassinate Nasser was suspected by the Brotherhood. This led to the regime acting against the Brotherhood, executing Brotherhood leaders on 9 December in 1954. The Brotherhood was banned and this time thousands of its members were imprisoned, many of them held for years in prisons and concentration camps, and tortured. On February 12, 1949 in Cairo, al'Banna who was a Freemason, was assassinated.

The influence of Freemasonry in Egypt and Arab countries struggling with post-colonial revolutionary sentiment cannot be overlooked. Hanna Abi Rashid, chief of the masonic lodge in Beirut, wrote:
"Jamaluddin al'Afghani was the chief of the masonic lodge in Egypt, which had about three hundred members, most of whom were scholars and state officials. After him, the leading master Muhammad 'Abduh became the chief. 'Abduh was a leading freemason. No one can deny that he has spread the masonic spirit in Arab countries." [Da'irat al'maarif al'masoniyya, p. 197, Beirut, 1381/1961.] *"As revealed by Abduh, al'Afghani developed in his students a practical inclination: he encouraged them to engage in the publication of magazines, to put in motion a current of opinion and to join, like he himself did, the masonic lodges of French inspiration."* (Tariq Ramadan, Aux Sources du Renouveau musulman, D'al-Alfghani a Hassan al'Banna un siecle de reformisme islamique, Paris: 1998, p. 54)
"At the same time Afghani started to introduce himself into the French circles of freemasonry. He introduced, as we have seen, the Egyptian intellectuals of his entourage who were to be, later, the principal actors of the 'Urabi Revolution. These circles had a crucial importance for al-Afghani: not only because they allowed him to

spread his ideas but also because he was able to meet with influential people in the political environment. Thus we can affirm, without any doubt, that this is the period, in which al'Afghani, thanks to the recognition and to the personal engagement in the creation of an associative body conceived on the model of the masonic circles, was able to accentuate his involvement in establishing political influence and alliance with the powers." (ibid., p. 85)

"In this period Afghani came forward as a political figure in two ways: by using a Freemasonic lodge as a vehicle for political intrigue and change, and by influencing people through oratory." (Ali Rahnema, Pioneers of Islamic Revival, London: 1979, p. 17) *"The Documents corroborate and help to date Afghani's membership and activity in the freemasons of Egypt....Most discussions of Afghani's masonic activity begin it in 1877 or 1878, but the Documents include a letter from him applying for membership in a masonic lodge which dates from the spring of 1875 and a note saying he had entered a lodge in Muharram 1293/February 1876. Unfortunately the name or rite of the lodge is not included. The Documents also include invitations to sessions of Italian lodges from early 1877 through 1879 and documents beginning in January 1877, from the Eastern Star Lodge, which was affiliated with the Grand Lodge of England....The lodge, with al'Afghani as its leader, was to become an important instrument in the growing Egyptian crisis of 1878 and 1879."* (Nikki R. Keddie, Sayyid Jamaluddin al'Afghani," Berkeley: 1972, p. 92)

After the attempted assassination of Nasser in 1954, the Egyptian government used the incident to justify political oppression of the Muslim Brotherhood, imprisoning a young Sayyid Qutb and many members for their vocal opposition to the Nasser regime. Mohammed Qutb, Sayyid's brother, along with other prisoners in the Muslim Brotherhood, took political refuge under CIA sponsorship in Saudi Arabia following Nasser's crackdown.

He was given different official positions at Saudi universities to teach and to carry out the mission of the Muslim Brotherhood. While in Saudi Arabia, Mohammed Qutb conceived of the organization now known as the World Assembly of Muslim Youth (WAMY), which was established in 1972, thanks to large donations from the wealthy Saudi bin Laden family.

Sayyid Qutb synchronized the core theological doctrines of modern Islamic theology: the Kharijites' *takfir*, ibn Taymiyyah's fatwas and social prescriptions, Rashid Rida's Salafism, Mawdudi's concept of the contemporary *jahiliyya* and Hassan al 'Banna's political activism. Mohammed Qutb taught at Mecca's Umm al'Qura University, and King Abdul'aziz University in Jeddah.

One of his fellow students was an aspiring Egyptian doctor, Ayman al 'Zawahiri. He eventually became one of Egyptian Islamic Jihad's strategic managers and recruiter. While attending King Abdul Aziz University in Jeddah, Osama bin Laden also became acquainted with Mohammed Qutb, and initiated into the Muslim Brotherhood. In 1979, Bin Laden left Saudi Arabia, being one of the first Arabs to join mujahedeen fighting against Soviet invasion in Afghanistan.

Osama Bin Laden, at just twenty-two years of age, established the MAK, the *Maktab al'Khidamat*, or the Mujahedeen Services Bureau, based in Peshawar, Pakistan. George Bush Sr., as vice president under President Ronald Reagan, was in charge of the covert operations that supported the MAK. The MAK was nurtured by Pakistan's ISI, Inter-Services Intelligence, and linked up with Pakistan's Muslim Brotherhood organization, the *Jamaat-e Islami*, founded by Abul Ala Maududi, to recruit mujahedeen in Afghanistan. By the late 1980s, the *Maktab al'Khidamat* expanded in fifty countries around the world.

Osama bin Laden then recognized that prospective Mujahedeen of the *Maktab al'Khidamat* did not have any military or intelligence training, and established the *Bayt al'Ansar* in Peshawar, Pakistan as a central training base, or *al 'Qaeda*. After the American invasion of Afghanistan in 2001, and Iraq in 2003 in retaliation for the September 11 terrorist attacks, al 'Qaeda found itself decentralized and tactically disrupted.

Numerous operating cadres of al 'Qaeda were established in Iraq after the 2003 invasion, which subsequently splintered in ideological and tribal confederacies, forming "al 'Qaeda in Iraq." When the Syrian Civil War erupted full scale in 2011, various insurgents and their brigades fighting against Syrian President Bashar al 'Assad networked strategically with D'aesh organizations like "al 'Qaeda in Iraq." An extremist group calling itself "Islamic State in Iraq and the Levant" separated ideologically from al'Nusra, an al 'Qaeda affiliate fighting alongside the Free Syrian Army during the Syrian Civil War.

The ISIL has its origins in a Kurdish insurgent group, which formed after the 2003 U.S. invasion of Iraq and was headed by terrorist Abu Musca al-Zarqawi, who swore allegiance to al 'Qaeda in 2004 to form al-Qaeda in Iraq (AQI). After al-Zarqawi's death by a U.S. air raid in 2006, the surge of U.S. military operations in 2007 and the program of bribing Sunni tribesmen to renounce resistance against the American occupation, AQI experienced a period of decline, but rebounded after the start of the western regime change operation in Syria in 2011, when the leader, Abu Bakr al-Baghdadi, dispatched fighters for Jabhat al-Nusra while renaming his contingent in Iraq the Islamic State of Iraq (ISI).

In a press conference in August 2009 with Turkish Prime Minister Recep Tayyip Erdoğan and President Abdullah Gül, Sheikh Hamad bin Khalifa al-Thani, the ruler of Qatar, expressed his desire to route a pipeline across Syria to Turkey for exporting his country's vast liquid natural gas reserves. *"We are eager to have a gas pipeline from Qatar to Turkey,"* he exclaimed, and in pursuit of that goal, Qatar began aiding a foreign insurgency in Syria almost as soon as Muamar al-Gadhafi had been killed in Libya in October 2011. Previously, Qatar had played a key role in toppling the Libyan regime by supplying rebels with weapons, supplies and training.

In January 2012 on the CBS news program 60 Minutes, Sheikh Hamad bin Khalifa al-Thani publicly announced his desire to topple the Syrian government, declaring, "For such a situation to stop the killing…some troops should go to stop the killing." Then in February, Qatar's Prime Minister Hamad bin Jassim al-Thani affirmed, "We should do whatever is necessary to help the Syrian opposition], including giving them weapons to defend themselves." To that end and at the request of Saudi deputy foreign minister Prince Abdulaziz bin Abdullah al-Saud, a military command and control center was established in the Turkish city of Adana, which is home to the U.S. air base of Incirlik, a convenient location for forwarding Washington's "nonlethal" aid.

Naming three Kuwaitis as prime fundraisers for ISIL, U.S. Treasury Undersecretary David Cohen said, "Through fundraising appeals on social media and the use of financial networks, Shafi Al Ajmi, Hajaj Al Ajmi, and Al Anizi have been funding the terrorists fighting in Syria and Iraq." Besides the funds funneling through Kuwait, ISIL seems to be developing its own financial sector. Paul Sullivan, a Middle East specialist at Georgetown University in Washington, said, *"ISIL is developing in a vital oil, gas, and trade area of the world."* Previously, ISIL gained control of the former Conoco gas field at Deir al-Zor in Syria, and, according reliable estimates, was already netting about $8 million a month before recent territorial gains in Iraq.

Contrary to transforming terrorists into ideological participants, the U.S., along with its Saudi, Qatari, Turkish, and British allies, has created an out-of-control monster with upwards of 50,000 fighters controlling an area the size of Belgium. "What began in Syria during the spring of 2011 as a simple uprising by a few so-called rebels has blossomed into a brazen and bloody movement led by the Salafi cabal, housed in Saudi Arabia, Qatar, and Turkey, to topple not just the Syrian regime, but also Iraq and Lebanon," lamented Agha Shaukat Jafri.

In 1982 Oded Yinon, an Israeli journalist with links to the Israeli Foreign Ministry, wrote The Zionist Plan for the Middle East. The thesis proposed, "That all the Arab states should be broken down, by Israel, into small units" and the "dissolution of Syria and Iraq later on into ethnically or religiously unique areas such as in Lebanon, is Israel's primary target on the Eastern front in the long run." The destabilization of the Arab and Muslim states, Yinon suggested, would be accomplished from within by exploiting internal religious and ethnic sensibilities.

Former NSA and CIA agent Edward Snowden revealed that the leader of the Islamic State of Iraq and Syria Abu Bakr Al 'Baghdadi was trained in Israel, Iran Fars News Agency, and Al 'Alam reported on exclusive leaked cache of ISIL precursors including their operatives and command structure as Israeli Mossad and U.S. intelligence assets.

D'aesh leader Abu Bakr al Baghdadi reportedly was a "civilian internee" at Camp Bucca, a U.S. military detention facility near Umm Qasr, Iraq. James Skylar Gerrond, a former U.S. Air Force security forces officer and a compound commander at Camp Bucca in 2006 and 2007, said the camp "created a pressure cooker for extremism." "Circumstantial evidence suggests that al-Baghdadi may have been mind-controlled while held prisoner by the US military in Iraq," writes Dr. Kevin Barrett.

In July Nabil Na'eem, founder of the Islamic Democratic Jihad Party and former top al 'Qaeda commander, told the Beirut-based pan-Arab TV station al-Maydeen all current al 'Qaeda affiliates, including ISIS, work for the C.I.A. American and British Intelligence agencies collaborated with the Israeli Mossad to create a terrorist organization that is able to attract all extremists of the world to one place, using a strategy called "the hornet's nest."

Extremism and fundamentalism in any religious guise, must never replace our experience of divine perfection and beauty. The divine intervention in the cave on Mount Hira is the mystic seal in a long mysterious tradition of Allah's intervention with humankind. Across the history of humankind, men, and women in cultures long-gone and empires whose ruins and exploits remain, have received mystic intercessions from Allah, encouraging us to enact goodwill, unconditional love, and morality. Far too often have these intercessions fallen to ridicule, linguistic misinterpretation (in the case of Christianity), becoming tools of war. *Humankind must separate the grace of God's Mystery and religion from the wicked acts of twisted minds.*

Sufis are the link in the biography of humankind that has made Islam the world's second-largest and fastest growing religion, with 1.2 billion adherents. Not a sect of Islam, Sufis are heirs of a nameless faith, hidden within both the Sunni and Shia branches of Islam, Sufis have through the centuries combined their secrets with the defense and expansion of Islamic mysticism. Sufis are both mystics and elite soldiers, dervishes and preachers, philanthropists and social workers; Sufis have always been in the vanguard of enlightenment and syncretic faith.

Without understanding the esoteric roots of the Sufis, we cannot understand the origins of contemporary political undercurrents in the Middle East. For radical fundamentalists like the Saudi Wahhabiyya and the Taliban, the Sufis are deadly enemies, who draw on mystical practices alien to the Quran. Where fundamentalist Muslims like Ayatollah Ruhollah Khomeini, and secular Baathist dictators like Saddam Hussein, Bashar al 'Assad, and Muammar Gadhafi rose to power, Sufis were persecuted and driven underground. For many mainstream Muslims, Sufism is simply part of the air they breathe. Engineering global peace is not contingent on a decline or secularization of Islam, but a renewal and strengthening of the antique faith, safeguarded by evanescent Sufis.

The Muslim Brotherhood was founded by a Freemason, Sheikh Hasan al'Banna. The *Bayt al'Ansar* or *al 'Qaeda* was established by American counter-intelligence CIA incentives under the direction of President Bush. The founders of *al 'Qaeda*, Osama Bin Laden, and Abdullah Yusuf Azzam operated under American counter-intelligence liaisons. Cadres of public officials, financial executives of major global financial institutions like the Financial Stability Board, International Monetary Fund, and Bank for International Settlements, and European consuls assumed total control of all fraternal societies in the European Union and United States.

Sectarianism sold out the syncretism of the antique faith that was parented by Arabian Magi and Sufi theologians centuries before the charters of the first Free Mason lodges. The terrorists that carried out the September 11 attacks, the very same mujahedeen that waged guerilla warfare against Soviet invasion during the 1980s, were bankrolled by the Central Intelligence Agency, and the Bank of Credit and Commerce International founded by Pakistani financier Agha Hasan Abedi, himself a Freemason and occultist.

BCCI launched an international monopoly with its purchase in 1976 of 85% of the Banque de Commerce et Placements (BCP) of

Geneva, Switzerland. After the BCCI liquidated this bank, it installed Alfred Hartmann as chief executive. Hartmann then became the chief financial officer for BCC Holding and was affiliated with the Rothschild family, sitting on the board of directors of N.M. Rothschild & Sons, London, and president of Rothschild Bank AG of Zurich.

BCCI was initially incorporated in Luxembourg, famous for its lax banking restrictions, and soon branches and holding companies sprouted up around the globe: in the Cayman Islands, the Netherlands Antilles, Hong Kong, Abu Dhabi, and Washington DC. BCCI's main route of investment was financing Israeli arms into Afghanistan during the Soviet invasion.

Our generation is revolutionary; the 2010 protests in Iran, the 2011 revolutions that changed political dynamics in the Middle East created a cultural conversion to a global community. Paramedia, and the development of artificial intelligence and noetic sciences, will enact revolutionary changes in social strata and technology that will rupture the fabric of human emotion and artistic expression. Now more than ever, the revolutionary youthful generations must make their voices heard in the name of freedom, social justice, and peace.

The wayward paths of disbelief in the divine Creator, Artist, Architect, and Causer of the universe lead humankind to emotional and spiritual darkness. The whisperers of witchcraft and occultism view religion as obsolete and destitute; would they surrender the human condition to endless spiritual anarchy? Prodigious minds contributed throughout the centuries to the pillars of art, classics, literature, music, and the sciences; they are the custodians of the Nameless Faith, a spiritual Cabal of enlightenment and artistic understanding of the human condition and humankind's destiny. These prodigies are found in Christian, Muslim, Buddhist, and other mystic world religious foundations. Coincidently, the sneaking whisperers (Surah 114) would see centuries of untold enlightenment in religious classics, arts, & literature, committed to diabolical ruin. The only alternative is interfaith dialogue, and self-awareness in God's grace – a true exclusive path to peace.

VIII. Regenerating Islamic Faith

The abject failure by the various schools of *'ilm al-kalam* (science of discourse) to create for Islam a secure niche among the religious sciences, or to renew a philosophical system independent of religious dogma, was not merely the result of the arrogant elitism of the Mu'tazilites and political opportunism. A deeper malaise afflicted the schools of logic, reflected in their methodological confusion and, simultaneously, their unrelenting zealotry. Ironically, it was left to the traditionalist theologians, notably al-Ash'ari, Al-Ghazzālī, and Ibn Taymiyya, to introduce some healthy empiricism into the theology by revealing some of the more glaring self-contradictions of zealous Salafist dogmas.

Traditionalists inherited some of the confusion of their theological opponents and fostered some of their own misconstrued conclusions. The confusion in *'ilm al-kalam* was the uncritical acceptance by all schools of kalam of the Neoplatonic premise that the perfection of God as an eternal being meant that he could not be the locus of free will and created things which has no beginning, we may also call it infinite regression (*hawadith*), while rejecting its logical consequence: God's remoteness from his creation and the impossibility of his day-to-day intercession with it.

Pioneers of the modern Islamic revival, such as Jamal al-Din al-Afghani and Muhammad 'Abduh, tried to revive Islamic philosophy and *'ilm al-kalam*; al-Afghani indeed insisted that the revival of Islamic philosophy and mysticism was an indispensable precondition for any revival. In the 21st century, the tides of revival in Salafism and Wahhabism have drowned all attempts at philosophizing and mystical examination. Consequently, the vibrancy and capacity for regeneration of the Islamic faith seem to be resistant to the emergence of scientific theologies and philosophies.

Reverts both spiritually independent, and active in their native religious upbringing become attracted to Islamic philosophy and science striving to discover answers to questions unanswered by science and their current state. What is the character and general structure of the universe in which we live? Is there a permanent element in the constitution of this universe? How are we related to it? What place do we occupy in it, and what is the kind of conduct that befits the spaces and planes we occupy? These questions are common to religion, philosophy, and higher poetry.

Islam is not an exclusively social and legal affair; it is neither mere thought, nor mere feeling, nor mere action; it is an expression of the Mystery and beauty of creation. Al-Ghazzālī, finding no hope in analytic 'ilm al-kalam, moved to mystical thought, and there found an independent context for religion. In this way, he succeeded in securing for religion the means to coexist independently with science and metaphysics.

A revelation of the Infinite in mystic experience convinced Al-Ghazzālī of the futility and inconclusiveness of *'ilm al-kalam* and drove him to a crucible between empirical thought and intuition. He failed to see that empiricism and mystical experience are organically related and that thought stimulates *taqdir* and inconclusiveness because of its alliance with space and time.

The main purpose of the Qu'ran is to awaken humans' higher consciousness of our manifold relations with Allah, s.w.t., and the universe. In spite of the zealous satisfaction on the part of Islamic orthodoxy, on the grounds that history has condemned or at the least ignored the mystical systems rejected by Islam as flawed and confused, there must be a regeneration of a viable worldview and a defensible theology, which could remain fallible and incomplete but still an essential guide for life.

A revert finding his, or herself overwhelmed in Islam's rich yet confused history of scientific and mystical thought could ask what, then, according to the Qu'ran, is the character of the universe which humans inhabit? In the first place, it is not the result of a mere creative accident:
"We have not created the Heavens and the earth and whatever is between them in sport. We have not created them but for a serious end: but the greater part of them understand it not." (44:38)

Allah's creation is a scientific wonder to be reckoned with:
"Verily in the creation of the Heavens and of the earth, and in the succession of the night and of the day, are signs for men of understanding; who, standing and sitting and reclining, bear God in mind and reflect on the creation of the Heavens and of the earth, and say: "Oh, our Lord! Thou hast not created this in vain" (3: 190-91). Again, the universe is so artistically designed that it is capable of extension: *"Allah adds to His creation what He wills."* (35: 1).

Creation is not a finite universe, a finished product, immobile and incapable of change. Deep in the universe's inner being lies the mysterious dream of a new birth: *"Say– go through the earth and see how God hath brought forth all creation; hereafter will He give it another birth."* (29:20). The point of these verses is that humans are endowed with the faculty of naming and forming concepts of Allah's creation, and forming concepts of them is understanding them. Humankind's knowledge is conceptual, steeped in empiricism and it is with the weapon of this knowledge that we gaze in wonder at the observable aspect of Allah's Reality.

The Qu'ran reminds us of this observable aspect of Reality by emphasizing: "
Assuredly, in the creation of the Heavens and of the earth; and in the alternation of night and day; and in the ships which pass through the sea with what is useful to man; and in the rain which God sendeth down from Heaven, giving life to the earth after its death, and scattering over it all kinds of cattle; and in the change of the winds, and in the clouds that are made to do service between the Heavens and the earth– are signs for those who "understand." (2:164).
"And it is He Who hath ordained for you that ye may be guided

thereby in the darkness of the land and of the sea! Clear have We made Our signs to "men of knowledge." And it is He Who hath created you of one breath, and hath provided you an abode and resting place (in the womb). Clear have We made Our signs for "men of insight!" And it is He Who sendeth down rain from Heaven: and We bring forth by it the buds of all the plants and from them bring We forth the green foliage, and the close-growing grain, and palm trees with sheaths of clustering dates, and gardens of grapes, and the olive, and the pomegranate, like and unlike. Look you on their fruits when they ripen. Truly herein are signs unto people who believe." (6: 97-99).

"Hast thou not seen how thy Lord lengthens out the shadow? Had He pleased He had made it motionless. But We made the sun to be its guide; then draw it in unto Us with easy in drawing." (25: 45-46). *Can they not look up to the clouds, how they are created; and to the Heaven how it is upraised; and to the mountains how they are rooted, and to the earth how it is outspread?"* (88: 17-20).

"And among His signs are the creation of the Heavens and of the earth, and your variety of tongues and colours. Herein truly are signs for all men." (30: 22).

The immediate purpose of the Qu'ran in observing Allah's immanence to Nature is to awaken in humans a consciousness of that where Nature is regarded a living symbol reflective of Allah's, s.w.t., power. We must note the general empirical context of the Qu'ran that engenders in Muslims a feeling of reverence and ultimately made Muslims pioneers of modern science.

The Qu'ran says: *"God created all things and assigned to each its destiny."* The *taqdir* of a thing then is not an unrelenting fate working from without like a taskmaster; it is the inward measure of what Allah has created, its realizable possibilities that lay deep within the depths of its inner being, and without any feeling of compulsion. Islam reveals to us that the universe is not a thing but an act. Knowledge of our *qadr* (destiny) however limited to human imagination gives us a direct revelation of the ultimate nature of Allah's Reality.

The Qu'ran infers that the ultimate nature of Realty is spiritual, and must be conceived as spiritual. Yet the message of Islam can reach us in higher aspirations than that of philosophy. Philosophy is an intellectual grasp of things; based in hypotheses and often falls short of reconciling spirituality with science. Philosophy sees Reality from a distance as it were. Religion seeks an intimate contact with Reality apart from theoretical hypotheses. Islam approaches the human condition as living experience, destiny sought for, an intimacy with the First Cause and intercessor of spirituality given to humankind. The scientific observer of Nature's *taqdir* is a mystic seeker in the act of prayer.

Prayer, then, in Islam made by individual or congregational in the Mosque, is an articulation of human inner longing for a response in the unfathomable silence of the universe. The moral and ethical injunctions of the Qu'ran appeal to the failure of man's ego and character, a failure remedied by prayer and meditation. *Jahannam* (blazing fire), therefore, as conceived by the Qur'an, is not exclusively an abyss of everlasting horror and despair inflicted by a revengeful God; it is a corrective prison, that makes a hardened ego once more sensitive to the living light of Allah's, s.w.t. Divine Grace.

Jannah (paradise) then, is not a holiday for the soul. Life is one and continuous. Muslims must regenerate their faith from uncompromising ideological traps of politics to receive ever-fresh illuminations from Allah's Infinite Reality that every moment appears in a new glory in Allah's s.w.t., Divine Grace. And, the recipient of Divine illumination in Islam is not merely a passive recipient. Every act of a free will creates a new *taqdir*, enacting further possibilities of creative destinies.

Truly, the Qur'an regards both *Anfus* (self) and *Āfāq* (world) as intimate sources of knowledge. God reveals spiritual signs in inner as well as outer mystical experience, and it is the duty of Muslims to examine the knowledge-yielding crucible of mystical experience. The function of Sufism in Islam to make sense of mystic experience; draw the Muslim closer to God through acts of remembrance and praise; though Ibn Khaldūn was the only Muslim who approached it in a steadily scientific spirit.

Science is the most momentous contribution of Arab civilization to the modern world, but its fruits were slow in ripening, now in danger of being overshadowed by ideological divergence. The syncretism of Sufism and Islam provides us with a shining example of the logical and religious genius of Islam - a panorama of continued tensions and challenges and of equally persistent efforts to resolve these ideological tensions and meet these challenges in a process of social regeneration and adaption to an Islam without political intrigue. It would seem that if Islam is to continue as a living faith, *'ilm al-kalam* (or something like it) may need to be regenerated, so that progressive Muslim self-understanding, interrupted some six centuries or so ago, can be renewed.

Sufism is an Islamic path that allows the human to reach Allah's grace in the here and now, in the present moment; through orthodox worship (salat, *dhikr*, *Ramadan*), art, meditation, and love. It opens doors of perception and scientific inquiry, or inspirations to, our deepest levels of existence, our purpose of life (*qadr*), and future of human civilization. The mystic path in Islam is synchronous with other mystical traditions makes the knowledge of Allah's s.w.t. divine grace possible.

Sufism is a living tradition and its legacy is a long and reputable, systematic approach to sciences, psychology, cosmology, pneumatology, and even holistic medicine. The all-encompassing Islamic tradition includes systemic treatises on Qu'ran and Hadith, prose letters, volumes of poetic masterpieces (*Mathnawi*), the nature of reality and the mind, epistemology, ontology, and vast literary classic treasures in varieties of language. Sufi writings include some of the most profound insights on love, divine grace and the relationship of the two with human nature.

Sufi poets and artists speak to us from across the boundaries of time and culture. The rich history and culture of Islamic poetry, music, and art in Sufi traditions has the power to evoke a spiritual state in the souls of non-Muslims, even in those not ordinary inclined to religion. The power of music and art in religion, especially in Sufi Islam is ecumenical; sacred in all cultures. Sufism makes its music and sacred calligraphy vehicles for the flight of the soul to Allah, s.w.t.

Sufism historically and presently is opposed by two forces in Arab society. Reactionary secularists and radical zealot Islamic revival movements essentially were ideological polemics, and yet part of the same anti-spiritual polemic that opposed Islamic mysticism. No more evident of ideological extremism in the form of Arab nationalism is Kemal Ataturk's Turkey. Ataturk banned Sufi orders, imprisoning and killing many Sufi teachers. Wahhabism is the other reactionary force persecuting Islamic Sufism in every country their institutions breed radical and zealous intolerance. The Salafist and Wahhabist counterparts sought to overcome fifteen centuries of rich Islamic history, music, art, philosophy, and sciences; persecuting non-Muslims, Sufis, any human souls not meeting their aberrant interpretation of the Qu'ran.

Despite attempts by Pan-Arab nationalist and Wahhabist-Salafist zealots at undermining Islamic mysticism, Sufism has become the spiritual antidote for both these aberrations. Sufism remains alive and accessible to the sincere revert of Islam. Souls who revert to Islam and enter the Sufi tradition practice it fully and religiously. There are souls who are devout in the spiritual paths of their own religious systems, essentially Christianity and Judaism, but synchronize methods of Sufism like chanting, meditation as some Christians and Jews have done so from Yoga and Zen. The syncretic nature of Sufism regenerates lost elements in a souls own religion, aiding in the recovery and rediscovery of Allah's s.w.t., Divine Grace.

Sufism is a sacred science, *al-'ilm al-a'lā*, a syncretic science that through calligraphy and art, music, pneumatology, psychology, and cosmology investigates Allah's s.w.t., Divine Grace. In Sufism, the entire created universe and the human soul is seen in relation to Allah s.w.t., and Oneness, *wahdat al'wujūd*. The created universe for the Sufi is regenerated every moment (*tajdīd al-khalq*). The writings of Rumi, Shams-i-Tabrīz, Hafīz, and ibn'Arabi abound with the diverse sacred sciences, art, and spiritual hermeneutics of Sufism.

Sufism represents a common delineation between the subconscious mind and religion. Islam needs a regeneration of faith, for a freedom of ideas, intolerance against cruelty, hypocrisy, and religious persecution; an opposition was to injustice and political crime. Stories, art, music, and poetry in Islamic mystic schools remain the subject of divine intoxication, love, and human suffering. Sufism is syncretic merging the triumphant characters of the human story with Divine Grace.

Islamic mysticism defies fortunes of the Caliphates, outliving the world's calamities. They are an eternal school surviving all empires, conquerors, kings, and revolutions. Sufism is a comfort to the broken hearted, immortalizing the artist, consoling the soul's silent calamities. Sufis are saints of the Highest Caliber, a light for lost souls, and guides of the bewildered. Sufi Islam has proved in times of political oppression to be a light of safety and hope for such a hopeless time. A True Symbol of the immensity of the Reality of Allah and Divine Grace. Reviver of the human soul, supporter of Truth.

As Ibn 'Arabi stated,
"My heart has become capable of every form: it is a pasture for gazelles and a convent for Christians and a temple for idols and the pilgrims Ka'ba and the tables of the Torah, and the book of the Koran. I follow the religion of Love: whatever way Love's camels take, that is my religion and faith."

Art illustrations and cover: © Hamid Nasir 2015

Born in 1965, Pakistani artist Hamid Nasir started painting from an early age. At that time, there were numerous prominent artists including the old master Allah-Bux in the city of Wazeerabad (Gujranwala), which provided a good nurturing environment for the arts.

Hamid Nasir is best known for his calligraphy using fine hand Urdu script called the Nastaleeq. During this time, he executed several landscape and portrait works using various medium. Greatly inspired by the famous calligraphy artist Sadqain, he looked for new inventive ways to represent colour through observing several works from the famous and renowned calligraphic artists.

Hamid Nasir feels that the art of calligraphy has enabled him to connect to the unspoken secrets of life, and while his art has progressed day to day, he still feels that the vastness of the art of calligraphy makes him realize that knowledge of the written word is infinite and limitless.

Research Bibliography

Iqbal, Sir Muhammad *The Reconstruction Of Religious Thought In Islam*. New Delhi, India. Kitab Bhavan, 2000

Qutb, Sayyid. *Islam: The Religion of the Future*. Kuwait: The Holy Koran Publishing House, 1984.

Qutb, Sayyid. *Milestones*. Indianapolis: American Trust Publications, 1990.

Qutb, Sayyid. *Social Justice in Islam*. (Translated by John B. Hardie & Hamid Algar) New York: Islamic Publications International, 2000.

Nasr, Seyyed Hossein, *Sufi Essays (London: George Allen and Unwin Ltd., 1972)*

www.ingramcontent.com/pod-product-compliance
Lightning Source LLC
Chambersburg PA
CBHW040329300426
44113CB00020B/2703